SEARCHING *for*
HOME

SEARCHING *for*
HOME

SPIRITUALITY FOR
RESTLESS SOULS

M. CRAIG BARNES

Brazos Press
A Division of Baker Book House Co
Grand Rapids, Michigan 49516

© 2003 by M. Craig Barnes

Published by Brazos Press
a division of Baker Book House Company
P.O. Box 6287, Grand Rapids, MI 49516-6287
www.brazospress.com

Printed in the United States of America

Library of Congress Cataloging-in-Publication Data
Barnes, M. Craig.
    Searching for home : spirituality for restless souls / M. Craig Barnes.
        p.   cm.
    Includes bibliographical references.
    ISBN 1-58743-062-2 (cloth)
    1. Spiritual life—Christianity. I. Title.
BV4501.3.B37 2003
248.4—dc21   2003009265

For my brother Gary,
who was with me on the road

Contents

Midway along the journey of our life
   I woke to find myself in a dark wood,
   for I had wandered off from the straight path.

How hard it is to tell what it was like,
   this wood of wilderness, savage and stubborn
   (the thought of it brings back all of my old fears),

a bitter place! Death could scarce be bitterer.
   But if I would show the good that came of it
   I must talk about things other than the good.

How I entered there I cannot truly say,
   I had become so sleepy at the moment
   when I first strayed, leaving the path of truth . . .[1]

Dante, The Inferno, I. 1–12, p. 76

Homeless

Lost in the Search for a Good Place

The sun was shining hard on my father's coffin as it lay perched above the hole in the ground where he would finally stay put.

We were standing in one of those stark cemeteries that don't have any trees. The grave markers were tarnished little plaques that lie low on their backs just below the grass line, so it wouldn't be hard for the guys who mow the brown lawn. Dad had spent most of his life in the shadows, so I knew he would hate this place and be eager to join those hiding under the ground, protected from the revealing light.

He spent the first part of his life trying to be at home in the respectable places. Not only was he the head of our home, but he was also the head of our home church, serving as the pastor. But failing at all of that, he left when I was a teenager. For almost thirty years I never knew where he was as he abandoned all who loved him. He abandoned every notion of home to roam about as a tourist through life. He died alone on Thanksgiving, 2000. At the time he was living in a raggedy Airstream camping trailer parked at the

9

"Mobile Home Village" somewhere in the middle of Florida. We buried him a few miles down the road.

If it were up to him, and for the first time it wasn't, he wouldn't have shown up for this funeral. But there he was. So dead, and yet finally so present. It was one last pathetic irony in the life of a father known mostly through absence.

People driving by the cemetery on the other side of the rusted chain-link fence slowed down to take a look at the bereaved: my older brother from Dallas, my aunt from somewhere in Virginia, my wife and me who lived in Maryland, and a handful of people from the trailer park. It occurred to me that no one belonged here—least of all my father.

I was never sure about where home was for my dad, but I knew this wasn't it. Burying him "a few miles down the road" may have been the perfect symbol for his meandering life, but it was still a lonely one. We imagine that our loved ones will one day be placed under a large oak tree on a grassy knoll not far from the family homestead. That way even their graves will tether us to the home where our souls are always nurtured and our identities renewed. But my father is now resting near the highway somewhere in the middle of nowhere.

Standing beside that barren grave, watching the dry wind toy with a piece of litter along the road, I wondered if this was the identity to which I was tethered. I had never thought about home much before that afternoon, but since then it has been my great passion. What is home? Where is mine? And how do we conduct lives that amount to something more than getting a few miles on down the road to nowhere special?

MEMORIES OF HOPE

Shortly after Dad rolled into town, a few months earlier, he met the minister performing the graveside ceremony. He was the one who called to tell me my father was dead. But he didn't know Dad any better than anyone else who had brushed his life, so he just said all of the appropriate and forgettable things that ministers say at a time like this. When he got done, he smiled tenderly and went down the line shaking hands with those of us sitting on the green plastic folding chairs. Then he took his place beside the colorless man in the dark suit who ran the local funeral parlor out of the first floor of his house.

Although we hadn't planned on it, my brother and I accepted the minister's invitation to "Say a few words." I think I said something sentimental about looking forward to meeting my Dad on the other side where we could finally settle down together. I really don't remember. What is vivid in my mind are the gentle tears that made my brother pause in his comments. He started out so well, just like Dad would have done, holding an open Bible as he spoke. But in the middle of one of his respectful sentences, the tears interrupted. So he just stood there, the eldest son beside his prodigal father's casket, unable to keep saying a few words about the father whose presence had also been interrupted. It was the only thing about the funeral that made sense.

After the service was over, we milled around a bit until the harsh sun finally won and we shuffled off to the rental car. Driving away, from the rearview mirror I watched the grave diggers crank the casket down into the earth.

The woman who managed the trailer park had asked us to stop by on our way back to the airport in order to see if there was anything we wanted from our father's small trailer. I was horrified at the thought and said, "No thank you, we really need to be going." So she asked my dutiful brother who said, "Sure," which meant I'd get to enter Dad's little hell on wheels after all. It was the kind of trailer you have to stoop down to enter, like when you're walking into a small airplane. I wondered what it would be like to live in a place where you can never stand tall. Dad's few possessions were neatly organized, placed into little compartments hidden under the sofa, above the bed, and along the walls. Each compartment had a little latch that would keep things safely inside for when he had to hit the road again. The metaphors were overwhelming. Quickly, I opened every cabinet searching for the place where we had traveled with Dad through all his wanderings. Then I found it. In an old, three-ring, leather notebook.

I remembered the notebook from my childhood. Dad had used it to work on his sermons back in the days when he was a Baptist preacher. For eight years he led that small church on Long Island that our family literally built, brick by brick. Since it was the place where my brother and I had spent our formative years, it was very much our home. Though I doubt it was ever his.

As a child, sitting beside him in the car on the way home from a worship service, I would pick up the notebook from the seat and gently leaf through the sermon notes that had just come from the pulpit. I thought I was holding the Ten Commandments. Funny how he had walked away from everything and everyone in his old life except that notebook.

"Why did he keep this?" I asked, plopping down on the little sofa in Dad's trailer. The pages were filled with new contributions to his old Bible studies, mostly from Paul's Epistle to the Romans. Always Romans. Dad liked his theology beefy. I was reassured to know that in all his meanderings through life, he had apparently never tried to walk away from his God. So he died still believing in some of the things he used to preach—things that had molded the faith of his two sons, who are now both ordained.

Some of the pages were hard to read, like those where he had scrawled out his shame for telling people he was the pastor he no longer was. We had heard rumors that Dad had spent time down South charming his way into rural congregations as a traveling evangelist, but as soon as his reputation caught up with him, he would ramble on to the next town. His notes on sin were filled with remorse for wasting so many years moving from one deception to the next. As I turned the pages of the notebook, I was amazed by how hard he had been on himself over the years. It never really occurred to me that Dad had been chased by such relentless shame.

As overwhelming as all that was, it was the end of the old notebook that made my heart stop. Across the top of a fresh page was written, "Daily Prayer List." The first two names on the list belonged to my brother and me. A bit further down he had even included the name of our mother, his long-divorced wife. I had assumed that Dad had forgotten us, or that when it came to the mental file marked "family," he had somehow found a way to press "delete." But we were there, in his prayers, on his last day.

Over the years my brother and I had sent so many letters to places he had just left. All our phone calls to the latest Dad-sighting were always met with, "The number you have requested is no longer in service. No other information is available." We could never make him understand that we wanted him, needed him, in our lives. He missed all of the weddings, graduations, births of his grandchildren. Somehow it was hardest of all that he missed our ordinations, and now I knew he would never even hear me preach.

Half of all marriages end in divorce. As painful as that is, I understand that at times it can't be helped. I also understand that divorcing a spouse doesn't mean abandoning children. Maybe Dad understood that as well, and the guilt kept him from us. No longer in service.

So I suppose it was this guilt and shame that prevented him from reaching back to us, even when he knew he was dying. Maybe. But about this I am now sure: in the end, the memory of the Father's house was still with him.

Knowing that, I miss my Dad more than ever.

OUR FAVORITE LIE

For years I have rehearsed my favorite lie, telling myself that Dad was a strange anomaly and my life will never look like his. As comforting as that has been, I know it's not really true. Dad is but an extreme illustration of what has already happened to my own soul and pretty much every soul I care for as a pastor. We are lost. And nothing is harder than finding home again.

Most good therapists would tell me that my decision to enter the pastorate was a way of trying to find my father. That doesn't mean that I am not qualified, gifted, or even called by God to be a pastor. It does mean, according to the experts, that God used the brokenness of my family to set the agenda for my own ministry. I think they are partially right about that. Actually what I and most everyone I know are searching for is not just our fathers, but our lost home. But we're never going to find that place.

The real home for which we yearn isn't the place where we grew up or the new place we're hoping to build, but the place where we were created to live. Paradise. When Adam and Eve left the Garden of Eden, we are told that God placed an angel with a flaming sword at the eastern gate. It is the Bible's way of saying that all of life is now spent east of Eden. In other words, as the saying goes, we can't go home again. Paradise has been lost. The yearning for it is the only trace that remains.

We weren't created to roam about the earth lost and confused. We were created to live at home with God, which is what defines paradise. Like Adam and Eve, we didn't realize that at the time because there was something forbidden in the middle of the garden that we couldn't have. How could it be paradise, we wondered, if we do not have it all? It is striking that the creation narratives make a point of telling us that this forbidden fruit was in the midst of the garden and not off in some forgettable corner. This means we were created to live with an unavoidable reminder that home was never meant to be perfect, whole, or complete. That's God's idea of a good creation.[2] What was missing from the good garden was meant to serve as our altar of prayer, where we could bend our knees and confess that we were mere creatures who were never meant to have it all, but were dependent on our Creator, who alone is whole and complete. That pristine, sacred communion was precisely what made the garden so good.

As the story goes, a serpent convinced us that the good creation wasn't quite good enough and that we could be like God and have it all if we just made one little home improvement. It was the exact lie we were dying to believe. Literally. Since sacred communion can only exist in freedom, God gave us the freedom to either bow before him or to listen to the serpent and attempt to recreate the garden in our own image of goodness.

Today the serpent whispers in our ears that we have a right—one of our favorite words in contemporary society—to live without loneliness, yearning, or confusion about the future. "Take control," it hisses into our ears. "You won't get kicked out of the garden or end up like your parents." The lie always appeals to our deepest anxiety, and it's too appealing to resist.

Actually, we could have resisted but didn't, so now we can't. Which is what John Calvin was trying to say in his doctrine of human depravity. We've become junkies to the serpent's lie, and we keep believing that the next thing we reach for will make everything just right. It never does. This means we are completely incapable of saving ourselves or finding our way back to the good garden. In other words, we're lost.

This is not to say that we are lost to God, as if that were ever possible, but clearly we have lost our home in paradise. It doesn't matter how fervently the spiritualized among us protest that their souls have been saved, we all continue to wander through this life on the other side of the guarded gates of paradise, missing home.

If there is a hope of finding a home, and I fervently believe there is, it can't mean returning to Eden. The hope bids us to keep moving ahead. But it is the memory of Eden, written on every newborn soul, that makes us discontented with the place where we are. It may be nice, but it's no paradise.

HOMESICK

It doesn't matter where you move, how fast you run, or how many new identities you try on along the way, you can't escape the longing for home. Most people don't destroy their families and homes in order to die alone in an old camping trailer. Right. But we all leave home, and, like my Dad, we never recover from it.

Even if you stay in the same community in which you were raised, which is rather unusual today, you're stuck with the same longing the rest of us have because the community itself has changed. Sometimes it is we who leave home, sometimes it is home that leaves us, but an inescapable dynamic of life today is that we are a long way from where we used to be.

The only approximation we have of our true home with God is the place where we grew up. For some that was such a terrible place that the approximation is pale, and they never want to return there. For others the childhood home was a place filled with delightful memories for which they are thankful, but from which they are not trying to recover. They've moved on. But in either case leaving home as a young adult sets an agenda in our souls to find a new place where we belong.

According to the U. S. Census Bureau about 43 million Americans move in an average year.[3] That accounts for 16 percent of the population who are hitting the road every year. And for the most part it's a different 16 percent that move the next year, and a different group the year after that. Pretty soon the numbers add up. The typical American is now expected to move fourteen times over the course of his or her life.[4]

Why are so many of us constantly moving from one place to another? If you ask people that question, and I have certainly asked plenty, the most common answer involves work. As the geographer David Sopher has claimed, "It is the property of vegetables to remain rooted."[5] Our society has taught us from an early age to move ahead in life, and after going away to college we discover that our next move is getting the best job we can, and then an even better job, and then a better one after that. These jobs are usually all in different places. Work may be the excuse for our transiency, and it may even be the only reason of which we are consciously aware. But the pastor in me has been digging deeper to discover what is it that drives us to accept these job offers that make us pack up and take off again.

The answer of the Scriptures to this deeper question is that from the beginning we have been searching for paradise. We think that the next place, where a more lucrative job is waiting, will afford us a better chance of creating it for ourselves. But it never quite works out that way. The house may be bigger, but we were never really looking for that. We're looking for home.

Before long the new place into which we have moved is marred by all of the pressures that we thought we had left behind in the old one. Stress always seems to be conveyed from one house to the next. In our disillusionment, we find other ways of distracting ourselves and staying on the move, even though our address has not yet changed.

Francis Mayes, a university professor who lives in San Francisco, responded to her divorce by purchasing an old house in the countryside of Tuscany, Italy. She wrote a popular book called *Under the Tuscan Sun: At Home in Italy* about her adventures in renovating the house, called Bramasole, which means "to yearn for." Often the book describes the frustrations of having to leave Bramasole to return to her life in San Francisco, where she spends nine months a year. This means much more of her time is spent away from the place she yearns for than in it, which is pretty descriptive for all of us.

In one of the most telling chapters of the book, she describes her observations of the many friends who stop by to see her Tuscan house on their way. As is typical of American tourists, they crammed in far too many stops in their travels, never spending much time in one place, and thus, never getting to know the places along the way. After seeing this repeated pattern, she concluded, "It's not the destinations; it's the ability to be on the road, happy trails, out where no one knows or understands or cares about all of the deviling things that have been weighing you down, keeping you frantic as a lizard with a rock on its tail."[6] Eventually, however, we run out of trips and other distractions from the deviling things of life. That's usually about the time we decided just to move again and look for another rock under which to place our tails.

Quite a bit of literature has been published lately by sociologists and cultural observers who are fascinated by our transiency.[7] One of the most popular of these, written by Gary Pindell, is called *A Good Place to Live: America's Last Migration.* Pindell's thesis is that now people are no longer willing to live anywhere the job calls, and given such recent technological advances as telecommuting, it is no longer necessary. Now, he claims, people are more interested in finding a "good place" in which to settle down. The good place has main streets with grocery and hardware stores you can walk to, and perhaps bump into your neighbors along the way. It hasn't been wrecked by developers, strip malls on busy four-lane boulevards, and the endless sprawl of ugly houses that all look alike. We've had it. We're sick of it. And we are looking for a good place again. But the reader doesn't get too far into the book before wondering if the "last migration" to a good place doesn't look an awful lot like the migration of the Cleaver family to their suburban home in the 1950s.

Pindell illustrates the search for a good place with his own life. After painting an almost idyllic description of his community in Keene, New Hampshire, complete with the white-steepled church on the village green, he decided that it wasn't quite good enough. As he says, "Fully cognizant that there were lots of places in North America far worse than Keene, I set out to see if I could find better ones. . . ."[8] He soon discovered his search was common to thousands who were all using the same short list of towns. So he organized his book by chapters describing fourteen "good places"—towns ranging from Asheville to Santa Fe. The fascinating thing about his descriptions is that there was something wrong with all of them. Right. Exactly right.

That's because we're yearning for home, and home has nothing to do with how good the place is. It has everything to do with whether or not it is the right place. And the right place isn't something you choose, but a place that chooses you, molds you, and tells you who you are.

SEARCHING FOR THE RIGHT PLACE

The longing for home isn't always expressed as such. When my parishioners come into my office to talk about the issues of their lives, they will often describe their frustrations with a marriage, children, or the lack of these things in their lives. Or they may want to talk about their calling in life, or their overwhelming grief over a loved one who has died. But these are only the most available of their emotions and desires. Just behind these perceived needs is the deeper longing to get to the place where life seems right again.

That is what home is; it's the right place, the place where we belong, where we know who we are, whose we are, and are no longer bothered by the revealing light as my father was. That's paradise. It is not a perfect place and it never was, even in Eden, if by that we mean nothing is missing. But at home life feels just so right. That's because it is a place where the sacred communion has been restored and made right.

This is what the Bible means by the term *righteous*. It has nothing to do with our piety and everything to do with restoring all of life to the right place where it was created to dwell. As Jesus futilely tried to explain to the Pharisees, nothing will prevent you from finding home quite like your pietistic reassurances that you couldn't possibly be lost.

I am constantly amazed by the number of Christians I meet who really have no need of Christ. Oh, they may admit that Jesus' death on the cross was important to their salvation, but that's pretty much an historical event in their thinking. Now they act as if Jesus offered them nothing more than a second chance to be righteous all on their own. But it doesn't matter how many chances we get, returning to the right place with God or anyone else is exactly what we are incapable of doing all on our own. It is only those who know they are lost who are waiting and hoping for a Savior to lead them to the right place. Home.

None of us know where the right place is, let alone how to get there. We're just clear that this isn't quite it. We may not even know how it happened, but we lost our way searching for it. And even though we have never been there, we miss it like crazy. So we are always homesick.

Earlier in my pastorate I used to peddle a lot of advice hoping that it would show people how to return to the right place. "Well, have you tried. . . ." I would often begin. They would always say, "Yes, of course," and so I would think of something else they should try. We would keep at it, until I would finally pull out my ministerial trump card and tell them to try more prayer. Then they would slink out of the office feeling worse than when they entered because I had just made it clear that their problems were an indictment on their inadequate prayers.

As misguided as this form of pastoral care was, it rose out of an intense desire to offer help. I truly loved these lost souls, and I wanted to do something to help them get out of the barren wilderness. Every minister I know nurtures the self-image of Moses, thinking it's our job to get people into the promised land. Since it's obvious that our parishioners are struggling in the wilderness, we want to get them out of this hard place and back to the right place as quickly as we can. So we come up with every shortcut to home that we can imagine. "Try prayer." I now realize that nothing could be more dangerous to their souls, because every short cut leads only to a mirage in the desert. There is no quick way to get to the right place, least of all prayer. The grace of prayer is that it allows us to commune with a righteous God who is on the journey with us. But it was the gracious decision of God to be with us that restores this communion and gives us some sense of home along the way.

No one in the Bible was ever asked by God to stay in the wilderness. The point of entering it is only to discover communion with the God who alone can bring us out of it and into the right place for us to dwell. But the promised land is different from paradise. We are eventually called to leave our desert wandering and enter into places where we will serve as priests to those around us, calling them to join us in building a righteous kingdom that will approximate, and never more than that, humanity's true home with

God. That is the best home we can ever find. But no matter how right we become with God, we'll never succeed in talking our way past the guard at the east gate of Eden.

Actually, all of our righteous activity and praying has a way of making us all the more homesick. In prayer we confront the alienation that gnaws at our souls, and we confess that we have tried so many paths to get to a place where the gnawing will finally go away—marriage, law school, a new job, the stock market, even spirituality. But we didn't make it home before dark.

WALKING WITH DANTE

Dante Alighieri expressed this common universal predicament in the opening words of his *Divine Comedy*: "Midway along the journey of our life, I woke to find myself in a dark wood, for I had wandered off from the straight path."[9] The moment Dante was awakened to this frightening discovery he began his pilgrimage through the inferno of hell and the mountain climb of purgatory before he could at last find his way to the paradise for which his soul yearned.

The Divine Comedy consists of three books of poems: *The Innferno, Purgatory,* and *Paradise.* Dante completed this classic in 1321, the year of his death, while he was a political exile from his beloved home in Florence. He knew he would never return home, and he missed it terribly. He would say that we never really leave home, but we carry at least the longing for it in our hearts. It's the longing that's important to him as it propels him along in the journey, not to Florence but to paradise. As the reader travels with Dante, who calls himself the pilgrim, it becomes clear that he is searching for a larger home than the one he left behind, a new home that can explain all of life on earth, including the lives of those who have grown accustomed to suffering beneath earth in the hell they have created.

Dante chose the title of *The Divine Comedy* for his journey home in order to contrast it with the tragedy plays that were still popular in his day. A tragedy, according to classical categories, depicts a plot that starts out wonderfully but ends in crisis. By contrast, a comedy begins in crisis and ends with redemption.

His entire journey as the pilgrim through hell, purgatory, and paradise happens over the course of one week beginning with Maundy Thursday, as a way of affirming that the events of betrayal, death, and the discovery of new life are at the heart of all of life. These christological categories become his means of interpreting our own betrayal of the paradise we were created to enjoy, the slow dying of the soul apart from its true home, and the gracious reach of God who finds the lost and dying and brings them to the new paradise, where they are at home forever.

Everything Dante writes about his journey through the afterlife is meant to provide insight into this life on earth. *The Divine Comedy* is not written as speculation about what may happen after death, and neither was he writing allegory like *Pilgrim's Progress,* in which Christian gets bogged down in the slew of despondency. Instead, Dante portrays real historical people, like us, whose lives are now seen in the light, or darkness, of their eternal significance.

In the following chapters of this book, Dante will serve as a guide in our search for home. His timeless poetry describes our longing for what was lost, our passion for what may be on the other side of the hell we know, and our fatigue along the way in the journey. With him we will discover how to reach that glorious place where we are finally at peace on earth because we are home with the Triune God who embraces both heaven and earth.

We begin simply by joining him in the confession that somehow we strayed from the straight path and have awakened to find ourselves in a dark wood. As Dante continues in the opening lines, "How I entered there I cannot truly say. I had become so sleepy at the moment when I first strayed, leaving the path of truth."[10] The most striking insight of these verses is that we were walking in our sleep when we went astray. If our eyes were opened we would have seen the detour for what it really is. Does anyone really believe that a little more money will lead them to the place of blessed contentment? No. But when we get tired and sleepy on the journey we entertain any ridiculous dream that isn't bothered by the rigorous daytime intrusions of truth.

Like Dante, it is easiest to wake up and confess the truth at the midpoint of life. By then we have made enough mistakes and tried enough short cuts out of the dark wilderness to realize we are far from the path of truth and are never going to find paradise on our own. Worse, by the time we approach the middle of life we discover that nothing we can do is ever going to atone for the sins we have committed along the way. We've done too many things we thought we were never capable of doing, and we have awakened to find ourselves in a dark wood of regret. By the middle of life we realize that we have already passed all the important choices. All that is left, we think, are consequences.

The greatest danger in the dark wood is not that we will become more lost trying to get to the right place, but that like my father we will grow accustomed to the darkness. The point of places that feel like purgatory is not to find a way to get comfortable there, but to refine our desires until we realize that we will only be at home with God. And the point of hell is to see the alternative.

TRACES OF GOD

Whether we want to admit it or not, the longing for home is welling up from the soul. This may even be the most enduring trace of God upon our lives. It's as basic to the biblical literature as Adam and Eve who long for paradise, Abraham who leaves home in order to find a promised land, the exiled Hebrews who are stunned to be stuck in Babylon, and the prodigal son to whom the memory of the father's house returns. The entire biblical story depicts men and women roaming from one disconnected experience to the next, unable to be at home where they are, uncertain that they will ever find where they ought to be. Eventually, we just built a tabernacle or a temple and occasionally worshiped a God who seemed far away.

But just as God was never one to settle or remain in exile, neither can he resist entering the dark wood to find us and join us on our nomadic, meandering journey. We thought that we were stuck in just another day through the purgatory or hell from which there is no escape. But from the perspective of heaven, there is purpose and even direction to our days. It may be hard, after all these years, to still believe that we are going to find any approximation of paradise on earth. But that is only because we have not trained our eyes to see the Sojourner God.

When we awaken to the identity of this one who is with us, we discover that paradise has found us, along the way. And in that rests all of our hope.

"Everywhere He reigns, and there He rules;
   there is His city, there is His high throne.
   Oh, happy the one he makes his citizen!"

And I said to him: "Poet, I beg of you,
   in the name of God, that God you never knew,
   save me from this evil place and worse,

lead me there to the place you spoke about
   that I may see the gate St. Peter guards
   and those whose anguish you have told me of."

Then he moved on, and I moved close behind him.

Dante, The Inferno, I. 127–36, p. 71

2

What Is Home?

A Place with Father, Son, and Spirit

When Dante began his journey through hell and purgatory to find his way home to paradise, he was accompanied by the Roman poet Virgil, who had been sent by heaven to serve as his guide. When Dante describes his great journey in *The Divine Comedy*, he too uses the form of poetry. That is because home is more easily found with the help of a poem than a map.

It isn't so much a geographical place as it is a place in the heart of God where we were created to dwell. When you find that home, all the other places of life start to make sense again.

T. S. Elliot, a more contemporary poet, wrote about our search for "the still point of the turning world . . . where past and future are gathered together."[1] Home is that still point. When you get there you know that you, and even the chaotic turning world, will again be right.

THE DARK DAY

September 11, 2001, was a hard day to be a pastor in Washington, D.C. I spent most of the day trying to find all of our parishioners who worked in the Pentagon.

Several of them had offices in the wing of the building that took the direct hit from the hijacked plane. An admiral who is a member of the church spent hours crawling out of the rubble, and a naval captain who teaches Sunday school was home at the time but lost everyone in his office. Our church treasurer was listed among the missing until late that night. Later we learned that he had just jumped up from his desk and run down the hall to a committee meeting for which he was late. As soon as he arrived he heard the explosion. He then ran back to find an airplane where his office used to be. So he threw himself into the relief efforts, which was why we couldn't find him. When we accounted for the last of our eleven members in the building, all alive, I breathed a sigh of relief thinking we had survived the crisis unscathed. How could I have been so wrong?

Few in the country were left unscathed by that dark day in our history. As we stared into our televisions that kept replaying video of the crumbling towers in New York and showing the gaping wound in the side of the Pentagon, we heard a legion of commentators tell us, "We will never be the same." At the time we didn't know exactly what that meant, but we knew it had to be true. It was particularly true in the nation's capital.

Over half of my congregation worked in government buildings, all of which suddenly felt like targets for terrorists. Parents began to take a little bit longer to get to work in the morning because they wanted to hug their children one more time, just in case.

Soon the anthrax scourge began. Eventually over thirty of our government buildings were infected, and we lost count of how many people we knew who were receiving the precautionary treatments. So the anxieties were sky high for months.

Actually the anxieties are always there. We are constantly dealing with low-grade anxieties about our jobs, marriages, children, health, and dreams that are in great peril. But in times of crisis these anxieties are harder to avoid. That is one of the thin slivers of grace that can always be found in a crisis—it makes it harder to ignore the subtle worries that drive our lives. In a crisis no one is still pretending that everything is just fine.

The terrorist attacks didn't just destroy our tall buildings and thousands of lives. They also destroyed the American assumption that we were not vulnerable to the atrocities most of the world has known for most of the history of human civilization. In the months since that dark day, most Americans have done all they can to get life back to normal. This is illustrated in the almost manic commitment of the construction workers who were determined to restore the Pentagon within one year to looking like nothing had ever happened to it. But some of us are wondering if all this resolve to return to normalcy isn't a way of missing the possibilities to redeem this horror by allowing our understanding of life to be transformed.

The reality is that our country was never as impregnable as we imagined, and neither is any individual home immune from the crises of diseases, divorce, and even violence. Until we take our place among the vulnerable peoples of the world we will nurture only an illusion about home. So it is wisest to take seriously the crisis moments of life. They are our best opportunities to discover the sacred activity of God, who is constantly inviting us to leave the home of our illusions, but only to move us closer to the true home he has prepared.

The philosopher Paul Ricoeur has written about the creative possibilities of what he calls a "limit experience."[2] That is an experience that takes us beyond the limits of normal life and calls into question our ability to comprehend life anymore. A limit experience is the one we spend most of life avoiding, dreading, defending ourselves against, because we think there is nothing beyond the limits of ordinary life but emptiness, loss, and anomie. But there is more. There is also a God whose capacity to recreate our home has no limits.

I did a lot of pastoral counseling in the days following September 11, but I soon discovered that what people wanted most of all was to worship. Their thirst for it was insatiable. In the week immediately following the terrorist attacks, we held a worship service just about every night, always with a full sanctuary. Prayer vigils, communion services, memorials—they didn't care how we put the service together, they just wanted to be in the house of the Lord. On Sunday we had the largest attendance in worship in the 206-year history of the church.

Why was worship so important in a time of national crisis? For the same reason that people ask the pastor to pray in the emergency room. Because when you're in trouble and beyond the limits of your own abilities, what you want most of all is to go home.

FINDING SANCTUARY

The late historian of religions Mircea Eliade claimed that all ancient religions cherish some type of *axis mundi,* or axle around which the world revolves.[3] To this day many tribal groups still build their homes around a single, sacred pole that extends spiritually through the center of the earth and into the heavens. The function of this pole is to keep heaven above and the earth beneath, for they are held together only by the *axis mundi.* A disaster was seen as a terrifying event because it meant that the earth was being removed (dis) from the stars (aster). Whenever disasters occur, people always run for protection beneath their *axis mundi* that keeps the heavens from falling on them.

Another historian of religions, Joseph Campbell, referred to the axial tree that can be found in all of the Native American religions.[4] This tree, he claimed, is the axial center of the four corners of the earth and the mystical place where the world is held together. From ancient to contemporary times all religious people have cherished some sacred symbol that nurtures their hope they are not abandoned to the anomie and chaos of life. This is what Christians are looking for when we gather on Sunday mornings beneath a cross—our axial tree, where heaven and earth are held together.

A few weeks after September 11, a woman in our congregation who works in the Pentagon told me that she was so shaken by what happened that she took a trip back to the farm in Alabama where she grew up. She said, "I went there to walk the ground on which I grew up, because I was hoping it would put the world back in order for me." I asked her, "Well, how did that work out for you?" "Not very well," she sighed. "No one really remembered me there, and besides, they were all just as scared as I was." So now she was sitting in church still confused and frightened.

As anyone who has tried it discovers, going back to the ground on which you were raised won't bring you home. So then you come to worship. As the confused, doubting disciples once said to Jesus, "Where else can we go? You alone have the words of life." We don't go to worship because we prefer to be there. We go because it's the last place on earth, the still place that binds the chaotic world to our true home.

In *The Divine Comedy,* shortly after the pilgrim awakens to the dark desperation of the wood in which he is lost, he's ready to hear Virgil's promises about God's control over all the earth, even the wood. The poet then promises to lead him to this place from which it can be seen that "Everywhere He reigns, and there He rules." Hearing that, the pilgrim begs the poet to show him this place that he may see for himself the gate St. Peter guards.

It is significant that it was important to Dante to state in the beginning of his three-volume work that the purpose for this pilgrimage is to see that God reigns not just in paradise, but everywhere. If the pilgrim can believe that, then he can also believe that he is saved from "this evil place." That is what a clear vision of the gates of St. Peter offers us. It is not only the entrance to our true home, but the *axis mundi* that reminds us no matter how evil or dark the world becomes we will still be saved because God reigns everywhere.

So the woman from Alabama had the right instinct to travel home in order to get life back in order. She just picked the wrong home. Seeing that now, she had come to worship to begin the journey to the only place that could restore meaning to her chaotic world.

When the disaster is so great that airplanes are falling out of the sky and towers are collapsing, the need for this *axis mundi* that binds earth to heaven is obvious. But in reality, we who trudge into church on Sunday mornings have always been walking on shaky ground. Our jobs, relationships, and health are never as secure as we think, and eventually we realize it is only a matter of time before we lose all these things. Scared, or at least anxious, we enter the sanctuary of church like children who run home with skinned knees.

When people come to worship, I don't tell them "Welcome home!" That's what they want to hear, and why they rush to the sanctuary in times of disaster. Some preachers tell their congregation that their new home is with the new family, the church. However, even in the most spiritualized sense of the term home, this isn't quite right. More accurately what we should say is that in the church you found long-lost brothers and sisters who are as confused about home as you are.

As one who spends an unforgivable amount of time in churches, trust me on this—if church is the home we have been looking for, we're in bigger trouble than we thought.

Worship is the means by which we renew our longing for the true home. Good worship has to confess both how much we long for home and how lost we have become in our search for it. Thus the point of worship is not to find home but to become more clear about exactly what home it is we are yearning to find.

The search to find this home wells up from our souls and subtly drives most of our decision making. Like salmon who knock themselves out to leave the vast expanse of the ocean waters and find their home upstream, we too jump over one hurdle after another, hoping it will get us a step closer to the place we know we belong. The salmon are trying to get back to the place where they were spawned. They don't exactly remember the place in the way that humans remember home, but there's something inside them that just knows where they belong. Or at least they know where they don't belong, and they are on an upstream quest to get out of the ocean.

The city of Seattle has built a series of locks for the ships that are making their way to port. Alongside of these locks the city has also built a "salmon ladder," which is actually more of an underwater staircase. They've also constructed an underground walkway next to the ladder with windows against the water. This allows observers to watch these amazing fish as they fight against the strong current trying to jump to the next step. When I saw them I was amazed by how beaten and worn they looked. It's a lot of work trying to get home. The great majority never make it but die trying.

When we come to worship, our souls look a lot like these beat-up fish who have tried to climb back home. And so the first thing we have to do in worship is to confess that we're never going to make it. This is just one of the reasons the church has historically called its place of worship a sanctuary. One of the great services the church provides society is to be the unique place where we find sanctuary from all of the other means of salvation that peddle one more thing for us to try in the vain quest to get life to the right place.

WHAT HOME IS NOT

One of the greatest challenges to continuing our pilgrimage to the right place is that we are surrounded by so many mythologies about home. There may be as many myths as there are pilgrims, not the least of which is the mythology of those who don't think they have to be pilgrims but have already found their true home.

Below are some of the more prevailing myths contemporary society presents to us. None of them will suffice.

A Norman Rockwell Painting

It is impossible not to be inspired by the sentimental portrait of the large family sitting down to the Thanksgiving table as the mother places a huge turkey in front of them. That's exactly the home where we would all prefer to gather for the holidays. But that family doesn't exist, and the portrait is an unfortunate judgment upon the family we have.

Rockwell wasn't painting our family tables, but our aspirations of them. If he had wanted to give us a glimpse of the true family table it would have been stained with painful memories, a chair would have been vacant to remind the family of the loved one who recently died, and at least one person at the table wouldn't be able to smile. There isn't a family on earth that is spared any of these harsh realities.

The pain of how things really are at home makes the ambitious among us think that if we work real hard, marry the right person, and get our kids in good schools, we can make our family look Rockwellian. And it makes Christians think that if they read the right spiritual literature, follow the right prescriptions, and have family devotions, then God will make their family look like a Rockwell with an open Bible on the table. But there are no formulas, either secular or religious, that can prevent a family from being comprised of humans. To be human is to bring the wounds of our hurts home every time we sit at a family table. There's even enough hurt to pass around.

The Thanksgiving table is not our *axis mundi,* and when we try to make it that, the axle soon breaks under the heavy burden of disappointed expectations.

To find a more helpful portrait of the true family table, we would do better to look at Leonardo da Vinci's painting of the Last Supper. There we see the images of grief, confusion, pending separation, and betrayal—but also a Savior in the midst of it all who bears the burdens.

A Painful Place

While some of us are motivated by a particularly stylized and sentimental notion of home, like that portrayed by Rockwell, others of us are overwhelmed by a dark and painful one. For these people, home is the last place they want to go. Usually this is because they collected too much hurt from the place where they grew up, and they really don't care for more. So they avoid building new homes. They may live in a house, and even raise a family, but every time they are expected to act like this is their home, they will only sabotage their own efforts. To do otherwise would open them to more hurt, and they're just all filled up on that.

As a pastor, I have never ceased to be amazed at the vast numbers of people whose memories of their childhood are not at all warm. When they have to visit their aging parents, they always do so more out of obligation than anything remotely resembling delightful homecomings. Even the knowledge that they ought to forgive and find freedom from the past misery doesn't seem to help because there is a big difference between insight and change. I have found that painful memories of home comprise the most difficult area of life for my parishioners to find redemption, and thus they are the most dangerous to their future.

The great danger of living with a painful notion of home is that our face is always turned backwards. We can't really see how to move ahead to the new home because we are preoccupied with the heartaches of the past. The danger is not only to our new home, but also to our souls. To assume that home must be a painful place just because it once was is not only to settle for victimization, but also to tell the risen Savior that we would prefer to remain in the tomb. But on this side of Easter the door to the tomb is open, and the Savior can no longer be found inside it.

The Wonderful Place Where You Grew Up

The further we move away from the home of our childhood, and the longer we stay away, the more idealized home becomes for some of us. Like the Norman Rockwell painting, this too will become a judgment on all the other places that we are given along the way. The new house will never look quite as nice as the one in which you were raised, the Christmas tree will never be quite as spectacular, and the spouse will never measure up to the parent that was supposedly left behind. As Dante discovered in the second circle of hell, "There is no greater pain than to remember in our present grief past happiness."[5] And yet, when the "Lady of Grace" appears to Dante early in his frightening pilgrimage through a place he would rather not go, she introduces herself as the one "who urges you to go."[6] That's because there is no way to find home without leaving home. It is a grace to be told to go.

If you keep referring to the place of your childhood as home, you'll never leave home, which is a necessary step in leaving childhood. The place you were raised is not your home. It never was. At best it was a pale approximation of the real home for which you yearn deep in your soul. God alone can lead you there. But to get to that sacred place you have to leave the pale approximation behind, not geographically but emotionally. Even if you stay in your "hometown," even if you never leave the house into which you were born, it is still necessary to detach from the childhood illusion that this is the place where you belong. It is the only way the soul will be free to search for its true home with the Holy Family of Father, Son, and Spirit. To refuse that journey is to commit idolatry.

When Abraham was called to follow God's rather vague promise of being led to a new place, his first step was to leave Ur of the Chaldeans. "Now the Lord said to Abram, 'Go from your country and your kindred and your father's house to the land that I will show you. I will make of you a great nation, and I will bless you, and make your name great, so that you will be a blessing.'"[7] There was something about that promise of a blessing that made Abraham leave everything behind to chase after it. It was something only God could give him, and it couldn't be received in the father's house. So the first step in finding that blessing is to leave. If not physically, then we must leave behind the futile agenda of turning our parents' house into our blessing. The heart isn't actually yearning for familiarity. It is yearning for God.

It was for this reason that, through the prophet Jeremiah, God told the Hebrews living in exile to stop pining away for Jerusalem. "But seek the welfare of the city where I have sent you into exile, and pray to the Lord on its behalf, for in its welfare you will find your welfare."[8] It is precisely when we are not where we want to be, where we feel unknown, uncomfortable, and not at home, that our souls are opened to receiving the blessed gift of being at home with God.

"Where I Hang My Hat"

This phrase is often used by those who are trying to put as happy a face as they can on their meandering existence. They know they are a long way from the place where they were raised and from all of the places where they have encamped along the way. They have no illusions that the next place is where they will permanently settle, but they cannot live with the sad resignation that they will never be at home. So they look at the tent in which they are dwelling and call it home. But in the depths of their soul they know this apartment or new house with a five-year adjustable rate mortgage just doesn't really feel like home.

While serving as a pastor in Washington, D.C., I constantly met people who came from some other place and assumed they would only be in town for a few years before moving on to the next place. By the time they got to our town, they had piled up so many moves that many of them no longer even tried to make roots in the place where they were currently staying. Frequently they used this line about home being where they hang their hat, but by the time they used a few more sentences it was clear that the place their hat was hanging did nothing to salve the wounds of the soul created by our loss of paradise.

When people introduce themselves in Washington they will typically tell you their name, where they work, and then they will say something like, "I moved here three years ago from Kansas." Why do they paste that last clause in there? Because they want you to know that they are not at home here. Even if they have lived in the city for twenty years and have no real plans to return to Kansas, they can't help but say I'm really from someplace else. They might as well say, "I'm still not at home here." That would actually be more helpful to the soul's great desire to find its home, because the reality is that none of our souls are at home in the places we hang our hats.

As hard as it is to live with the yearning for home, at least the yearning nurtures hope. Those who are afraid to continue the search, to root themselves with a particular people, or to try to find even an approximation of the right place are doomed to despair. When Dante began his journey toward home, he first came upon the cowards who were kept for eternity in the vestibule of hell. That's because not even hell wants someone who was too afraid to try in life. Virgil describes their fate: "This wretched state of being is the fate of those sad souls who lived a life, but lived it with no blame and no praise. . . . Heaven to keep its beauty cast them out, but even hell itself would not receive them for fear the damned might glory of them . . . the world will not record their having been there."[9] Hell is the eternal home of those who made their home apart from God. But not even hell wants those who settled for the despair of life without a home.

It is significant that St. Benedict included a vow of stability in his rule for monks.[10] He was responding to the growing tendency of monks to wander about from monastery to monastery in search of something missing in the one just abandoned. He was also recovering a cherished sentence of counsel given by the early monastic tradition: "Sit in your cell, and it will teach you everything." What was meant by that phrase was that not until you commit yourself to a particular place will your prayers become the *axis mundi* that holds the whole world together. In your prayer cell you hang not only your hat but all of your hopes for finding home.

A Collection of Relationships

In response to the great transiency of contemporary society, many have stopped thinking about places and directed their longing for home toward relationships. This effort has the advantage of thinking about home in ways that are closer to the New Testament understanding than the geographical notions that belong more to the Old Testament. From its beginning the church has always thought about home more in terms of community than in land or stationary temples, and a community consists of relationships. In today's society, where travel and phone calls are cheap and e-mail is plenteous, it is possible to conduct community across all geographical barriers. At least that is how the argument goes. So why then are so many of us still feeling so lost when we have so many relationships scattered across the world?

The community that the New Testament calls us to enjoy is not simply a collection of cherished relationships. Rather it is a community rooted in communion with God. Apart from that fundamental constitutive element, all of our efforts at building community and fellowship with other transient Christians adds up to little more than what John Barth called "the floating opera of friends."[11] They come onto the stage of our lives for a while but all too soon float away. We resolve to keep in touch and stay close, but close is exactly what we are not.

New Testament faith is incarnational, which means that at some point there has to be a fleshing out of what we believe. To try to stay at home with friends through the Internet is to have nothing more than a virtual home. We have to be with those who comprise a part of our home. If that cannot happen through keeping our relationships in close proximity, and increasingly it can't, then it has to happen with the God who came in the flesh to be with us. But how do we commune with a God who is no longer in the flesh? Through the tangible elements of bread and wine at the family table where we meet our brothers and sisters from east and west, north and south.[12] But the family that gathers at that table comes only by the invitation of God. It is his creation, and without him it will always unravel.

AT HOME WITH THE TRIUNE GOD

Home is the place where we were created to live from eternity and for eternity—with our true Family of Father, Son, and Holy Spirit. All three persons of the Trinity were present at creation when the dark void and chaos that covered the earth was pushed aside by the Spirit, creating light and beauty. The word for Spirit in the Hebrew is *ruach*, which means wind, or the breath of God. When God created humanity, it wasn't until he breathed that holy *ruach* into the nostrils of Adam that he became a living being. Thus, from the beginning, the Spirit has been the source of our life.

We didn't make it to the third chapter of the great biblical story, however, before it became clear that humanity has an inclination to turn from its source of life back to the chaos. After Adam and Eve were banished from paradise, the story immediately turns into a dark tragedy that begins with one brother killing another and ends with Armageddon. That's because we always do the most desperate things when we are lost. The greatest tragedy isn't just that we keep killing each other, or that terrorists can fly planes into skyscrapers, but that along the way we have recreated the world to be a place where something dies within every one of us every day. That something is the *ruach*.

When Cain rose up against his brother Abel, he also destroyed the life within himself. The curse he received from God for his actions was two-fold. First, his work would not be fulfilling, "When you till the ground it will no longer yield to you its strength." Second, the Lord said, "You will be a fugitive and wanderer on the earth." From that day we have continued to replay the curse of this primal drama. We compulsively work at jobs we don't love but have to keep to afford lifestyles we really don't like either. And we wander. From one job to another, from one relationship to another, from one dream to another. We dare not stay too long with our disappointments.

Along the way we lose all but the faintest whisper of the life we were created to enjoy. After God had seen more of this than he could stand, he broke into the middle of the story to find us, restore us to life, and bring us home. That is why it is so important that when the Son was born among us in Jesus, he was conceived by the Holy Spirit. This is why the church has always looked to Jesus for the gift of life. Eternal life.

When Jesus was ready to begin his ministry he came upon a familiar scene where people were gathered on the banks of the Jordan River listening to John the Baptist, who warned them to repent before the Messiah comes. So the people would step into the Jordan and let John wash their sins away. But since we have long been addicted to our sins, it wasn't long before the people's lives would again be marred by the things that separate them from God. So the next week they would come back to the Jordan and try again.

When the Son of God insisted on being baptized by John, he was identifying with our futile efforts at getting life cleaned up. At that moment the Heavenly Father got so excited that he ripped back the clouds and claimed, "This is my beloved, with whom I am well pleased." Significantly, those words are not uttered until the Son identifies with us, which means the words were addressed to us as well. The lost had been found and called "beloved."

It was also at that moment that the Spirit descended upon the Son in the form of a dove. Then the Spirit drove the Son out into the wilderness where he was tempted as we were. When Jesus presented his credentials for ministry, he said, "The Spirit of God has anointed me to preach good news to the poor." Every day that Jesus walked our roads, felt our hunger, and took his place among those whose spirits had become poor in the search for home, the Spirit was pressing the incarnation deeper and deeper. In the work of the Son, through the power of the Spirit, the Father was finding us.

According to Paul, the Spirit continues to be about the holy business of adopting us into the Son's own beloved relationship with the Father. Just as the Spirit once drove Christ to us, so does that same Spirit drive us to Christ. This is why in Paul's letter to the Ephesians he calls us to live in Christ ten times in the first fourteen verses. It is because "in Christ" we have "received every spiritual blessing in heaven." All that heaven has to offer is already ours as the heirs of God and joint heirs with Christ.

What this means is that we are made a part of the Triune Family of Father, Son, and Spirit. That is our home. That is where we find life. It is where we belong, and we will never be content with any place other than that communion. And that is why we go to worship when the world is crashing down around us. Being in worship isn't the same thing as being at home. But it is our only way of calling home.

Such sweet decorum and such gentle grace
        attend my lady's greeting as she moves
        that lips can only tremble to name in silence,
        and eyes dare not attempt to gaze at her.
        Moving benignly, clothed in humility,
        untouched by all the praise along her way,
        she seems to be a creature come from Heaven
        to earth to manifest a miracle.

Miraculously gracious to behold,
        her sweetness reaches through the eyes, the heart
        (who has not felt this cannot understand)
        and from her lips it seems there moves a gracious
        spirit, so deeply loving that it glides
        into the souls of men, whispering: "Sigh!"[1]

Dante, La Vita Nuova, p. 56

3

Our Nomadic Meandering
How We Became So Confused

This sonnet, well known for its elegance, was written by Dante before he started *The Divine Comedy*. The reason it is so extraordinary is that the images and emotion are all about the beloved, and neither the lover or the love is typical of poems about passion.

It comes from *La Vita Nuova,* which is a collection of poetry Dante wrote to the love of his life, a woman named Beatrice. Dante met Bice, her real name, when they were children in Florence. He was always infatuated with her, but she was put off by his philandering ways as a young adult and refused to enter into a relationship with him. She later was married to someone else and died an early death. In his grief over this loss, Dante eventually idealized Bice as Beatrice, whose name means "bringer of blessings."

The poetry of *La Vita Nuova*, while written to describe the hard lessons of passions learned by a young man, prepares Dante for the mature theological claims made in the three books of *The Comedy*. In the *Vita,* Dante discovered the necessity of separating himself from the tradition of the Italian troubadours who were obsessed with love poems that focused on the pain of their unrequited loves. By contrast, Dante chose to focus not on his yearning but on his beloved Beatrice. In this he found his freedom from the pain of grief and past mistakes, and he found his guide, who in *The Comedy* would lead him home to the love of God.

In *The Divine Comedy* Beatrice reappears as a figure of grace who sends Virgil, the poet who also embodies rationality, to guide the pilgrim Dante through hell and purgatory. It is the lovely Beatrice herself, though, who ushers the pilgrim into paradise. According to the Thomistic theology of Dante's day, the grace of rationality and poetic insight into the soul can carry you up to the gates of heaven, but only sacred love can bring you all the way home.

Along the way in the journey through inferno and purgatory, Virgil is constantly appealing to the pilgrim to think more rationally, by which he means to focus not on his feelings and yearnings, but on their true goal. All of the souls of the damned that they encounter in hell are there precisely because they allowed their various yearnings to distract and even consume them until they became blind to the lost paradise that is the true origin of all desire. In his wonderful introduction to *The Inferno,* Mark Musa claims that Dante's point is that, "the man who would realize his poetic destiny must ruthlessly cut out of his heart the canker at its center, the canker that heart instinctively tends to cultivate."[2] The whole purpose of the pilgrim's journey through hell and purgatory is to get rid of this devilish canker that prevents us from entering our home, our destiny, in paradise.

Tragically, contemporary Western society has found many ways to distract us from the goal of the journey toward home. One of its favorite ways is to keep us preoccupied with our desire. Like the young Dante, we are more infatuated with our yearning than with its goal, and thus, more devoted to the search for the right place than with actually being there. So we wander from place to place, never really getting to know any of them because we no longer believe any place can really be right for us. What we believe in is the longing for our place.

It was not always this way. We have progressed as a society from the life of settlers to that of exiles and then to the meandering of nomads. But we were never at the right place.

SETTLERS

In my office hang six faded black and white photographs of rugged farm families. Each is sitting on the same rickety front porch of the dusty North Carolina tobacco farm they inherited from the family in the photograph before them. The last one is of my grandparents, Ada and Clarence Solomon Barnes, with their five children, including my father.

From the best of my research it appears that the first of these six generations immigrated from rural England and settled in the new land. But I could never get my grandmother to admit that. When she was still alive I once asked her where our family came from. She was a bit surprised by the question and said, "Well, North Carolina, of course, honey." I tried again. "But where did we come from before we arrived here?" "I don't know what you mean," she protested. "We've always lived right here on this farm."

None of the six families who worked that farm were confused about their place in this life. They had even rewritten their history to block out any memory that they used to belong to a different place.

When he was a young man my grandfather ran away from home to join the big bands, but it was a huge disaster that he despised, and the prodigal returned to the farm and was content never to leave it again. That wasn't because he felt "fulfilled" in his long back-breaking days on the farm, but because he knew in his bones that it was where he was supposed to be, like those who worked the farm before him.

Others who immigrated to America from Europe in later years often settled in urban areas and raised their families in ethnic neighborhoods where the old culture and the historic family identities were maintained. For a generation or two, leaving home meant moving out of the apartment but never the neighborhood where you were known.

After the Civil War, the emancipated African-American slaves did not all hop on trains bound for northern cities. For several generations most stayed in the land to which they had been dragged in chains because it was now the place that they knew. There they formed their own communities, built around the religion of the small frame church that had once been a symbol of the slave master's religion but had now been adopted and transformed as their own. Again, this wasn't because the conditions of life in the poor rural black communities was the best they could imagine, but it was the only economic option they were given. So they chose to make it home.

When Hispanics began to immigrate from the south, and Asians from the east, most were not running away from home as much as they were seeking work in order to send money back to the communities to which they hoped eventually to return. Like the Native Americans, the Hispanic communities in the southwestern part of the country weren't immigrants at all, but had been maintaining village life for centuries before manifest destiny overran them. When the railroads arrived (with the help of Asian immigrants), few were interested in jumping on board to head to the big cities back east. As with the other minority communities, that wasn't because home was a more comfortable place to live but because it was home.

For centuries and centuries this was the expected way of life all over the world. Home was where you lived, where your parents lived, and where your children were expected to remain. The settlers settled for that place because it was all they knew and all that was available to them.

These old homes of a bygone era were not easy places to be. The work was hard, the conveniences nonexistent, and human life didn't last long within them. At the close of the nineteenth century, the typical work week was sixty hours—if you were lucky enough to have work. Women worked a whole lot more than that just in their homes, not to mention the long days many spent in urban sweat shops or in the fields. Well over half the population was without indoor plumbing, which meant the family toilet was a hole in the backyard. The average life expectancy was about fifty-four years, which was just as well because few had pensions.[3] Toil and grief were as much a part of home life in my grandparent's house as the yellowed wallpaper that entombed them long before they died.

It was precisely this severity of life that nurtured a vision for a different place. While the settlers were clear about where their place was in this life, the religious among them just knew that there had to be a better place in the next life. So they spoke about heaven as their real home, which was waiting up ahead. This placement of heaven as being ahead of them is significant. They knew it wasn't behind them and it certainly wasn't with them. Even the most cursory review of sermons from this period reveals that heaven was presented as an eternal home for all who had remained faithful through their harsh life on earth.

It is also illustrated in the popular gospel hymns of their day. Typical of them is the old favorite, *In the Sweet By and By,* published in 1868.

There's a land that is fairer than day,
And by faith we can see it afar;
For the Father waits over the way
To prepare us a dwelling place there.

Refrain:
In the sweet by and by
We shall meet on that beautiful shore;
In the sweet by and by
We shall meet on that beautiful shore.

We shall sing on that beautiful shore
The melodious songs of the blest,
And our spirits shall sorrow no more
Not a sigh for the blessing of rest.

To our bountiful Father above
We will offer our tribute and praise;
For the glorious gift of His love
And the blessings that hallow our days.[4]

Bent over from the burdens of life, settlers all across the country gathered every Sunday into small churches to sing this favorite hymn that had found its way into the blood that pulsed through their hearts. In doing so they confessed their great hope. "We shall one day cross the river of death to meet on that beautiful shore, by faith we can see it afar, and when we get there our spirits shall sorrow no more." So maybe they weren't really settling. The hope of an eternal home, waiting up ahead, rose out of their weariness with the sorrowful home of this life.

It is the last line of this gospel hymn, however, that demonstrates a secret the settlers knew that subsequent generations have forgotten. The hope of heaven wasn't simply an escapist dream they nurtured. It was a means of finding sacredness in the days they had. That is the function of hope. It isn't about our fantasies for tomorrow, but about living in the day we have with a vision of how life ought to be and will be one day.

Thus the inspired vision of the future offers "the blessings that hallow our days" by placing the present in a larger, eternal context.

The Old Testament scholar Walter Brueggemann has demonstrated how the ancient Hebrews lived with this same understanding of hope tying together a future vision with the present reality. "Hope reminds us that the way things are is precarious and in jeopardy. Hope reminds us not to absolutize the present, not to take it too seriously, not to treat it too honorably, because it will not last."[5] But as the Hebrews and all the devout settlers after them discovered, hope provides more than a judgment upon the fleeting present. It also offers sanctification, bestowing eternal meaning upon the day in which it is found.

The settlers may have stayed where they believed they belonged, but only because they understood that as their calling for this life, not because it was the right place. For that they would have to wait until they arrived at that beautiful shore. For now, faith in that home up ahead made the home they had today right enough.

Although it didn't make a great splash in American society, it was during this era that theological liberalism was paramount in the thinking of European Christians. It advocated that through innate human potential it would be possible for the church to build the kingdom of God on earth. As profound and sophisticated as many of these theological claims became, they all shared something in common with pietistic American frontier religion—the belief that heaven was up ahead, and from that hope it was possible to inspire faithfulness and, as the liberals believed, progress in the day we have.

There were a great variety of theological and spiritual agendas by the early part of the twentieth century, but most of them nurtured in some form this vision of the heavenly home waiting just up ahead. It was their Beatrice, and like Dante they were more focused on it than their longing for it. That was the reason they lived with hope and were inspired with marvelous visions to labor another day, no matter how severe the work.

Not all of the American settlers gathered into those small frontier churches to nurture their faith that they would eventually cross the river into the right place. According to the most frequently quoted study, only about 17 percent of the population was actively associated with a church when the country was founded, and even by 1870 the numbers didn't rise above 35 percent.[6] Much of the growth that did occur was attributable to the evangelical renewal movement of the Second Great Awakening in general and the circuit-riding spread of Methodism in particular.[7] But in spite of this growth, the statistics reveal that for the first hundred years of the country's history the vast majority of its settlers avoided church.

Those who settled into their communities without an integrated hope of heaven had no heroic visions of a Savior and thus were forced to be their own heroes. It was for this reason that so much of the popular folklore from this era depicted idealized men like Davy Crocket and Daniel Boone, who battled the wilderness and triumphed over it, or gunslinging cowboys who had only their Smith and Wesson in which to place their hope. In essence, what these folk traditions claimed was that this is as good as it is going to get, and the strong and brave will go down fighting. That tradition has continued to persevere in the American heart every bit as much as the religious vision of hope. Maybe even more.

Recently a woman in our church buried her father, who was raised as a part of the settler generation. He had grown up in a particularly pietistic church, and by the time he left home had resolved that he would never force such phony piety upon his children. He had left not only the church but also the need for a Savior, which is pretty much at the core of Christian faith. This meant that, like the rest of his generation who avoided piety, he had to settle for himself as a savior. As she talked to me about her childhood, she recalled that in all of the stories he told his children, he was always the hero figure. He had to be, otherwise there is no moral and nothing redeeming about the story. This created an enormous burden upon the family, who knew better, and loved their father not as the hero, but because he was their dad. For example, she said, he always insisted on fairness. It was the most heroic moral he could find without a compelling vision of another home and another way of life that was drawn from a faith in heaven. Even his dying wish was that his ashes be split four ways between the children and sent to all of them. As she exclaimed to me, "It was always about mediating fairness with him. What child wants what is fair? I never wanted that. I've always wanted to be special to him."

Right. That is what every kid wants from the parent. And that is exactly what the voice from heaven tells us we are, when the skies opened up and the Father said, "This is my beloved." In Christ, we are even more than special. We are beloved. But we can only get that message from home.

EXILES

Society started to change when my father was a young man, and the settler generations gave way to new social phenomena. Technology, industry, education, and government all served as unwitting partners in calling my father's generation to leave the farm and the city neighborhoods. Chasing the promise of a better life, millions of young people took advantage of the GI Bill, got an education at a land grant university, then a job with one of the new corporations, and then settled their families in another new thing called suburbs, which were far from the old neighborhood or farm. But they never forgot where home was, and thus they were a generation of exiles.

The exiles were relatively happy living on the beautifully sculptured avenues of the new planned communities, in their new "all electric homes." But it is striking that every Christmas they would load up the station wagon and take the family home for the holidays. By that, they meant returning to the farm or the old neighborhoods for a visit. Exiles don't live at home, but they never forget where it is. If anything, they get a little nostalgic for the old home they left behind, remember it being nicer than it ever was, and never stay there long enough to remember the truth about its severity.

During this era, around the 1950s, religion in America began to flourish as a greater percentage of people attended church than ever before. Like government and industry, Protestant denominations became big business, with branch offices opening on the corners of every suburb in the country. At this time regular church attendance in America soared beyond that of the settlers, with some scholars putting the percentages as high as 69 percent of the population.[8] That is because unlike the Hebrews in Babylon, the American exiles really did want to "sing the Lord's song in a foreign land." As nice as it was to have matching avocado kitchen appliances, their souls still longed for the home they knew was someplace else.

The religious agenda of American churches in those days was to transform the romanticized childhood home that was behind the exiles into the heavenly home that was above them. Thus, while their parents thought of heaven as a future reward waiting up ahead, this generation relocated heaven up above the day they had. This is when we began to describe ourselves as a "nation under God," which is a notion that would never have occurred to our grandparents, and certainly not the nation's founding fathers.[9] Striving to make planned communities and all of society resemble the order and unity of the heavenly home above is classic exilic behavior.

During this era there was a resurgence of Augustinian studies, particularly noting his call to live as a citizen of the City of God while participating in the cities of earth.[10] It was also during this era that neo-orthodoxy burst on the theological stage, riveting the attention of all Western theological faculties. Its chief proponent, Karl Barth, swept away the vague liberal aspiration that society was somehow moving toward the new kingdom of God through its own progress. After society had witnessed the horrors of two world wars, no one found any theological claim based on the innate goodness and progress of humanity to be convincing. Instead, Barth claimed, our only hope is in the transcendent God's gracious decision to reveal his Word, Jesus Christ, who became flesh and dwelt among us. This contributed to the shift from thinking about heaven as the obtainable home ahead of us to now seeing it as the transcendent home of God above us. Revelation was no longer thought of as progressive, but vertical. Only by God's self-revelation in Christ can we get a glimpse of our true home. The exile generation's seminarians devoured neo-orthodoxy and graduated to preach about the "wholly other" God to their newly constructed and usually filled sanctuaries in the suburbs.

In addition to these theological indicators, perhaps the popular songs of the day are even more revealing. One of the favorites was *This World Is Not My Home*, published in 1946.

> *This world is not my home, I'm just a passing through*
> *My treasures are laid up somewhere beyond the blue*
> *The angels beckon me from heaven's open door*
> *And I can't feel at home in this world anymore.*
>
> *My Savior pardoned me from guilt and shame I know*
> *I'll trust his saving grace while traveling here below.*
> *I know he'll welcome me from heaven's open door*
> *And I can't feel at home in this world any more.*

I have a precious mother up in glory land
I don't expect to stop until I clasp her hand
For me she's waiting now at heaven's open door
And I can't feel at home in this world anymore

The saints in glory land are shouting victory
I want to join their band and live eternally
I hear the sweetest praise from heaven's open door
And I can't feel at home in this world anymore.[11]

"Somewhere beyond the blue" is our transcendent home. It is there that our true treasures lie, and not in the new Levittown house, the Chevy Impala in the driveway, or the annual two-week vacation to the Poconos. None of that does a thing for the person who finally has enough comfort to realize that the problem isn't the severity of work, but the severity of the soul. But by the forgiving mercy of God in Jesus Christ the door between the suburbs and heaven has been opened, and so we will "trust his saving grace while traveling here below." Having looked through that door, called Jesus Christ, we just "can't feel at home in this world anymore."

Like the settlers before them, since the religious among the exiles were clear about their real heaven beyond the blue, they were able to live with a reasonable amount of health and contentment. Their contentment was not in spite of the hardship, as it was with the settlers, nor was it because of their many comforts. It was because like the settlers they lived with a compelling vision of home. The clarity they had about the home above them was stronger than their disappointments that the good life wasn't quite good enough, and so they focused their lives vertically, lived in the places below, and did the best they could to make it reflect the home up above.

In spite of the fact that the majority of exiles were regularly attending church in the fifties and sixties, many did not. Those who had to cope with the malaise of exilic life without religious vision were destined to find their only meaning for life in suburban culture. But this was difficult, because inculcating one's meaning and purpose was exactly what the suburbs were not good at doing. What the suburbs were good at was keeping people on the move. The supermarket, another new invention, was way down the road and the Wal-Mart was in a different direction, as was the cineplex movie theater, the schools, work, and the tire dealership. (The whole notion of a tire dealership was new.) Typically none of them were nestled together on Main Street, as had been the custom for the settlers' neighborhoods. Further down the road from all of the new superstores and modern schools was that most blessed of new creations, the shopping mall.

There were a number of home-dismantling effects from all of this progress. One of the greatest of these was that the automobile became not only a necessity to get to all of these places, but a means of living in isolation from others.[12] The new suburban houses were built with garages but not porches, so it was possible, maybe even preferable, to come and go from one's house without ever having to stop and talk to the neighbors. Since it took so much time to get from one place to another, little was left for chatting with a neighbor you used to bump into on the sidewalk in front of the butcher's shop or bakery, not that either of those things existed in the 'burbs. Another effect of the planned suburban communities was that they failed to include what Ray Oldenburg has called "third places."[13] If a person's primary place is the house and secondary place is work, the third place they need in order to have a home, Oldenburg asserts, is somewhere to encounter old friends and make new ones. The English have pubs, the French have bistros, the Italians have piazzas, the Viennese have coffeehouses, and the Germans have biergartens. The closest thing the suburbs have to a third place is the shopping mall, but the cafe court isn't about community. It's about getting a quick fill up so you can return to consuming.

With the help of another new invention called the VISA card, eventually the exiles learned to shop and shop, until those new homes were jam-packed with stuff that could never really satisfy their insatiable appetites. That's because they weren't really looking for stuff. They were looking for home, but they could not turn their eyes up, so they looked only to the new products placed before them by a new profession called marketing. The marketers taught people how to do the very thing from which Dante struggled to find redemption—desiring desire. Quickly the exiles discovered that they had to work harder and harder to make their credit card payments. So now the exiles were stuck with jobs that they didn't really like but had to keep in order to afford a lifestyle they didn't much like either.

If that is all that the exile had, if there was no compelling vision of the right place up above and no means by which to critique and reorder life, then he or she was destined to discouragement with this life, and maybe even cynicism. And that is exactly the legacy inherited by the children of the exiles, who left the 'burbs and became nomads.

NOMADS

Unlike the exile, the nomad doesn't have a clue about where home is located, but simply wanders from place to place. Ask most people where home is now and you're likely to get a reflective pause while they think about their answer. They may list all of the places they lived as a child and then say, "But now my folks live in a retirement community in Florida." Or they'll say something sentimental about the cabin or beach house they try to get to once a year. What they are unlikely to say, if they are honest, is that they feel perfectly at home right where they are and can't imagine wanting to be anywhere else.

The increasingly common experience today is to wander through a world with very few borders. Recently my college-age daughter was studying in Europe. On her spring break she toured Hungary and Czechoslovakia. One sunny afternoon when she was in Budapest, she went to the ATM machine to draw money from her American bank account. She then used that money to pay for her meal at an Internet cafe, where she sent a note to one of her friends who was studying in Brazil. None of that seems extraordinary anymore, but in that little transaction she crossed numerous barriers that previous generations would never have dreamed of doing. When I was her age, growing up in the suburbs, Budapest was considered one of the bad places where you weren't allowed to go. There was even an iron curtain around it. As awful as the partitioning of Europe was, at least one of the benefits of knowing where you don't belong is that it helps you remember where you might belong. By contrast, all of the curtains and walls are down for her generation, which is a blessing. They can travel everywhere. Yet they don't belong anywhere.

Airports are no longer simply places where planes are parked; they have now become shopping malls and conference centers. After I returned from a business trip my wife asked me, "So how was Chicago?" "I dunno," I muttered, "It was a good meeting, but we never left the airport." We are living on the road.

Some say the teleconferencing technology will change all of this, creating the freedom for people to work without ever leaving home. Others say it is only creating a virtual work life that makes us virtually aliens to all geography.

Foreseeing a dangerous trend in our society that began with the exiles, Robert Kennedy once said,

> In far too many places—in pleasant suburbs as well as city streets—the home is a place to sleep and eat and watch television; but where it is located is not community. We live in too many places and so we live nowhere. Long ago Alexis de Tocqueville foresaw the fate of people without community: "Each of them living apart is a stranger to the fate of all the rest—his children and his private friends constitute to him the whole of mankind; as for the rest of his fellow citizens, he is close to them, but he seeks them not; he touches them but he feels them not . . . he may be said at any rate to have lost his country."[4]

A more contemporary illustration demonstrates how far the nomads have taken Kennedy's fears. The *Utne Reader* recently ran a lead article called, "Stranger in a Strange Land." It was written by an American living in Japan with his Japanese lover and her two kids who speak no English. He speaks no Japanese. He has clearly lost his country and is unable to be adopted by another. Being reminded every day of his alien status, the author writes, "The biggest challenge today is how to make peace with alienness."[5] But can that ever be done?

Being an alien nomad used to be considered difficult, but in postmodern society we have come to accept dislocation and disorientation as natural living conditions of those who have long grown accustomed to a fragmented identity. With Milan Kundera's "unbearable lightness of being," we slide easily from place to place, from identity to identity, which is precisely why the longing for home is greater than ever. After a while, usually around the middle point of life, all of the moves leave our souls tattered, worn-out, and lost in Dante's dark wood. We don't want another self-help book, exercise program, promotion, or even another intimate relationship. We just want to rest. But for that we need a home.

In a sense, the sins of the fathers have been visited upon the sons and grandsons. After our parents left the farms and the old urban neighborhoods, it was as if the gates to Eden were closed again and there is no way to return. So now we meander through our nomadic journeys still with the memory of our father's house on our souls, but without any idea where it is, let alone how to get there.

Clearly something happened in society to allow my father to be transformed from an exile to a nomad who spent the rest of his life wandering around. In earlier times, men and women may have abandoned the homestead, but it was a rare scandal to those who remained behind and wondered if the lost would return. Every message society used to give said, "Stay right where you are." By contrast, my father heard the message over and over again that he had to chase his dreams, even if he didn't have a clue about what they were. By the time he realized that he was longing for the exact place he left, he was too tired and confused to know how to get back there. And here's the important point—there was no back there. His home was gone. His wife had settled in another place with another man, and his sons were off wandering around looking for their own homes.

In recent years, some have tried to return to the simple life in the country, or to gentrify the cities, but these are neither large-scale migrations nor are they really successful in capturing what was lost when our parents left home. The new homes in the country are filled with conveniences our grandmothers never dreamed of, as well as fax machines, computers, and large-screen satellite televisions that all conspire to keep people away from the neighbors that were once a defining part of rural life. And the new condominiums downtown are hardly the kind of places where old women hang out of their windows all day and watch the kids play stickball on the street. But the effort to return to something illustrates the deep longing we all feel to find a place where our souls are at rest.

The devout settlers and exiles looked to heaven for that vision, which gave them a sense of meaning and even contentment in the homes that they had. It was not the paradise for which their souls yearned, but knowing where that home was allowed them to stay in the place they were living with a certain amount of contentment. But today heaven is neither ahead of us nor above us. Now only the elusive longing remains. And that is why we are homeless.

Sermons on heaven have been scarce in recent years. Occasionally a preacher will refer to it in a funeral homily, but it is very difficult to find a sustained preaching series on the topic from any contemporary pulpits. And systematic theologies of either heaven or hell are all but nonexistent.

Instead, what has riveted the attention of both preachers and theologians is relevancy to felt needs. Some do this by addressing therapeutic concerns and people's anxieties about relationships and the many stresses of life. Others address political and social agendas, and still others try to speak to the marginalized of society, giving us feminist theology, black theology, and liberation theology. The best of these theological agendas attempt to place their affirmations within a traditional confessional context, but all of them are seeking relevancy in a way that the Christian tradition has not known before. The old agenda was to make the individual or the particular community relevant to the inherited tradition. Putting it in the best light, this new concern about relevancy is an effort to further the reformation of the church to the changing cultural context in which it exists as God's mission to the world. But some of the old scholars are worried that the church is now doing exactly what the nonreligious settlers and exiles did by talking more about our yearnings than their object, namely, the Triune God.

As in previous eras, the popular music of the day provides some insight into the assumptions we now make about the relationship of our lives to home with God. One of the most telling is a song titled *One of Us,* which was released in 1996.

> *If God had a name, what would it be*
> *and would you call it to his face*
> *if you were faced with him in all his glory*
> *what would you ask if you had just one question*
>   *and yeah yeah God is great yeah yeah God is good*
>   *yeah yeah yeah yeah*

What if God was one of us, just a slob like one of us
just a stranger on the bus, trying to make his way home

If God had a face what would it look like
and would you want to see
if seeing meant that you would have to believe
in things like heaven and in Jesus and the saints and all the prophets

What if God was one of us, just a slob like one of us
just a stranger on the bus, trying to make his way home

He's trying to make his way home,
back up to heaven all alone
nobody calling on the phone,
except for the Pope maybe in Rome.[16]

The significance of this wildly popular song is that it demonstrates that we have abandoned any conviction about being settled in this life based on a clear and compelling vision of the heavenly home. The song begins with some traditional references to facing God in all of his glory, and even uses the lines from the traditional children's prayer affirming, "God is great. God is good. . . ." But it then moves quickly to the very nontraditional notion that wonders if God is just as lost as the rest of us, just another slob, a stranger on the bus, trying to make his way home. As sad as that would be, at least then God would be relevant.

When the song first came out I heard more than one devotional from a youth pastor using the lyrics as a contemporary paraphrase of the doctrine of the incarnation. But that is not what Joan Osborne is singing about. She isn't interested in describing how the Son of God left the splendors of heaven to become human in order to bring us home to the Father. She is more interested in claiming that God is just as alone as the rest of us "trying" to make his way home. If she can see that ordinary face, then she can believe, but "things like heaven and Jesus and the saints and the prophets" are pretty much beside the point.

As irrelevant as it may sound, things like heaven and Jesus are precisely the point for those who are lost and weary of their nomadic meandering. As the Son of God, Jesus Christ did indeed leave his home and become like one of us, but as he entered our streets and lives he maintained communion with his Father in Heaven and was thus never lost. Best of all, he sent the Holy Spirit, who adopts us into this beloved communion with the Father. Experiencing that, we too are never lost, and are transformed from wandering nomads into hopeful pilgrims who know the true object of our yearning.

I learned that to this place of punishment
all those who sin in lust have been condemned
those who make reason slave to appetite

and as the wings of starlings in the winter
bear them along in wide-spread, crowded flocks,
so does that wind propel the evil spirits

now here, then there, and up and down, it drives them
with never any hope to comfort them—
hope not of rest but even of suffering less.

Dante, *The Inferno,* V. 37–45, p. 110

4

The Alienated Nomadic Soul

The Danger of Being Homeless

There was a day when we were worried if the center could hold. But such anxieties are meaningless to the nomad who doesn't believe there is a center.

Without core beliefs holding their lives together, nomads float easily across the top of commitment, virtue, truth, responsibility, and community. Not belonging anywhere, they are not only nomads but aliens in every context.

They feel this alienation deep in their souls.

PARADISE LOST

Heaven and hell are not only destinations but also symbols of the eternal truth that are at the core of our lives whether we realize it or not. The point of the biblical authors was never to speculate about the afterlife, but to present just enough of a glimpse behind the curtain to inspire us to live with eternity in the day that we have. This is not to say that there aren't "real" places called heaven and hell where we abide for eternity. The New Testament is particularly clear in its conviction about that. But everything that the Bible says about the next life has the purpose of inspiring us to live out of an eternal vision for the life that we have today.

That is exactly how the previous generations perceived heaven and hell. These images offered a compelling vision of the right place where people knew they belonged—home. Until they arrived, their vision of heaven and hell was used to inspire, correct, warn, and guide their lives on the earthly journey. According to sociologist Peter Berger, images like heaven and hell historically provided cosmic significance to the earthly home. In his book *The Homeless Mind*, he has demonstrated that for premodern societies home was not only a place but also a religiously constructed center of the world that provided meaning and a sense of orientation to one's life. The medieval serf may not have had a particularly enviable lifestyle, but at least he didn't have confusion about his role or place in the larger world. His hovel of a house belonged on the lord's estate, and that meant that his home reminded him of his calling to serve his lord on earth, and thus, his Lord in heaven.

By contrast, Berger claims, in contemporary society these religious ideals have been dismantled and in their place individuals are only left with economic and bureaucratic means for constructing their lives.[1] In another book, *The Sacred Canopy*, Berger refers to this process as secularization. What he means by that term is that society is now attempting to hold together without resorting to common religious symbols that provide a unifying legitimation of its purposes.[2] To some degree this is only the logical effect of the modern infatuation with economic, technological, and bureaucratic structures of the last generation. In the 1950s we were devoted to corporations and government, which both got big about the same time, and we baptized them with various forms of civil religion. In other words, the function of many churches in those days was to nurture civility and the work ethic so that we might truly look like a nation under God. But eventually society began to see this baptism as a pretty empty symbol, and we simply maintained its faith in the secular structures without bothering to have them religiously legitimated.

Today we have largely lost faith even in the corporations and government, and we no longer trust them to unite us behind common purposes.

Instead we expect them to service the direction and purpose we are each discerning for ourselves. "You've got to believe in you," is the message the current generation has heard over and over. So now it is no longer religion nor the economic and bureaucratic structures that we believe in, but the individual. And the managers, not leaders, of corporations and government are knocking themselves out to give the individuals what they are demanding as their right. Actually, the corporate managers have always been more clever at this than those in government, and have found ways of convincing the individual what they should have by rights. As the DayTimer Corporation writes across the top of all their catalogues, "It is all about you."

The legacy of this is that many people now have comfort because of their economic means and security because of their privileged place in the bureaucratic structures of society, but frankly they are bored with their lives because they cannot find meaning in these things. That's because no one can find meaning in a self-constructed life, especially if there is nothing of eternity at the core. In spite of owning more possessions than the medieval serf would have dreamed of possessing, contemporary souls are empty. Which is just another reason why, like nomads, they wander through relationships, jobs, and a great variety of houses all in the mythological hope of stumbling into a home that offers to the individual the existential benefits that previous generations held in common.

It is because they belong nowhere that nomadic souls are always empty. You have to give yourself to a place before you can belong, and you have to belong before you can receive anything of eternal value from that place—things like the defining convictions for life.

The Loss of Self

When we shifted the center of all things to the individual, we were assuming that they knew who they were and what they wanted. But in the process of making this shift we removed individuals first from living under heaven and then from under the aspirations of a Great Society. Along the way individuals lost any means of knowing who they are or what they are about in life.

With nothing to inherit from the commonly held identity of the previous generation, now every individual bears the burden of constructing the "self." Parents don't tell their children what college to attend, but want only to help them decide for themselves. After arriving at college, students confront the need to pick a major, then another major if that one doesn't feel right. After graduation they have to pick a job, and when that isn't fulfilling, another job, and then another. Along the way enough economic resources are earned to be consumers of "goods" in the hopes of building a comfortable life. Once a person begins to construct his or her life through economic means, they assume the identity of being a consumer, and they consume not only things but also relationships, roles, jobs, and communities. But part of the definition of being a consumer is that one's identity is never satisfied, so they just keep consuming more and more, never able to adequately construct the good life.

In the very process of trying to construct a self, the individual becomes nothing more than a collection of roles defined by unrelated demands. The employer defines her by her production, her children's school as the PTA president, friends as a tennis partner, the bank as a good credit risk, politicians as a voter, church as the second alto in the choir, and the next-door neighbor as the lady who doesn't cut her grass often enough. There is no unifying center to her life, which means there is no sense of the true self that originates in her soul. Instead her life is actually being constructed by others, who all compete for her time, heart, and resources. She knocks herself out to succeed in all of the identities because they each offer her something. But this means her soul is for sale, so it is actually the consumer that is the consumed.

Ironically, in giving the individual the right and responsibility to construct life unencumbered by higher callings, we have only made it impossible for the individual to be anything other than the unintegrated construction of others. And we allow that to happen because, rather than inheriting an identity from above, we now struggle to maintain a plurality of identities, which results in having no true identity at all. In the words of Kenneth Gergen, "With post-modern consciousness begins the erasure of the category of self . . . we realize that who and what we are is not so much the result of our "personal essence" . . . but how we are constructed in various social groups. The initial stages of this consciousness result in a sense of the self as social con artist, manipulating images to achieve ends."[3] That's what happens when you lose your sense of home where you know who, and whose, you are.

The loss of this eternally grounded home has also left the nomads ideologically homeless with no compelling intellectual framework that even attempts to make sense of their life. Having abandoned heaven and hell and all of the moral guidance these images offer, they are left with just a series of experiences that defy evaluation. In his book *Girl-friend in a Coma*, Douglas Coupland, one of the nomadic literary voices, has recreated the tale of Rip Van Winkle. After falling into a coma in 1979, a young woman wakes up twenty years later. When asked about her impressions of the nineties, she responds, "A lack. A lack of convic-tions—of beliefs, of wisdom, or even of good old badness. No sorrow; no nothing. People—the people I knew—when I came back they only, well, *existed.* It was so sad."[4]

It is particularly troubling that cultural voices like Coupland, aided by all of the models of the J. Crew catalogue with blank stares, are trying to make this sadness cool. *New York Times* essayist Michiko Kakutani has called this "designer despair." She is referring to the popularity of Quen-tin Tarantino's cool-cat killers, Marilyn Manson's adolescent rage, and Jerry Springer's "South Park with real people." Most of us don't care to emulate these models, but their popularity rests on the nomadic recogni-tion of the absurdity of living without a compelling vision of life. While walking past a chic clothing store on a busy street one day, I looked inside to see a very large neon sign that presented a young man wearing no shirt and unzipped jeans. Across his bare chest were the words, "Romance is nice, but sex is really cool." Few people actually believe that. Even those whose moral base is slippery and ill-defined would still prefer romance to sex, but when the shocking becomes normative enough to sell a pair of blue jeans, it illustrates that nothing is really shocking anymore. That's because there is no such thing as "good old badness." But that means there is no such thing as good old goodness either. Traveling past so many neon messages of what is now cool, the nomads have no basis for evaluating if they are good or bad. Only cool.

THE LOSS OF COMMUNITY

Without a compelling vision of heaven, contemporary nomads are also destined to despair of finding anything that will offer a compelling vision of relationships, even though they long to find it, and they claim to take relationships seriously. But the best they are actually hoping for is to carve out a meaningful experience with somebody they care about. This is always tenuous, however. Abandoned to the burden of constructing oneself, the individual is always tempted to ask if a relationship is "meeting my needs," which is a radically new criteria for considering commitments. In the best of circumstances this is born out of intense loneliness and a desperation to find someone who truly understands one's internal conflicts and aspirations. But even then it still has the effect of commodifying relationships as one more thing to be consumed, which only contributes to the feelings of alienation and prevents anything remotely resembling the communion of souls.

It is even more difficult for individuals in search of getting their life together to express a comprehensive vision of community. They shudder at the thought of having to explain what their little experiences have to do with the absolute or eternal truths that bind people together under heaven, as they did for previous generations. Actually, the whole notion of an absolute truth sounds judgmental to the nomad who wants to honor other nomads by never saying more than, "I have found a little oasis with a few others, and it works for me." But the oasis doesn't really work, and it isn't long before the pseudo-community it offered evaporates like a mirage in the desert, leaving the nomadic soul lonely and empty once again. A community that is nothing more than a group of individuals, all with dreams for what they need it to be, isn't community at all. As Dietrich Bonhoeffer warned in *Life Together*, there is nothing more dangerous to authentic community than our dreams for it because we love those dreams more than the people around us. Community is not a human ideal, he says, but a divine reality.[5]

The divine reality is that we are often thrust together with people we don't particularly like and certainly don't resemble. But when that community has a common *axis mundi* at its center, it not only holds together but also holds heaven to earth. Since it is defined at the center, this community doesn't have to worry about boundary issues and can accommodate all sorts of diversity. That's because it holds together by having clarity about the center.

Ironically, by rejecting the whole concept of a religiously defined center as being too exclusive, the nomads wander into communities of their creation based on homogeneity that are defined not at the center but at the boundaries, and are thus very exclusive. So the leaders of a typical city now try to accommodate the interests of the various racial communities, the gay and lesbian community, the business community, and the religious community that is perceived as just one more gathering of individuals with common dreams. None of them look a lot like heaven on earth because the heavenly community has room for diversity. It was precisely because Dr. Martin Luther King Jr. had learned how to define our society at its center that he was able to inspire us all with his great dream of a color-blind society.

Having despaired of such lofty goals, the nomads of today seek rather to create their own little communities in ways that do not interfere too much with the pursuits of other little communities that define their individuality differently. We think that this makes us tolerant and pluralistic, but it actually only creates a society of subcommunities that are all alien to each other. And it reduces the function of these groups to buttressing the identity of the individual that comes to it out of fear of being perceived as alien by others.

The church is as bad at this as any other subcommunity in society. When I was a teenager the director of our youth group used to purposely schedule special Bible studies on the same nights the local high school was having a dance. We were told that this was all a part of our sanctification. "Come out from among them and be ye different." All it really accomplished was the creation of another subculture in our school. We were the kids who didn't dance, which felt okay as long you hung out with other kids who didn't dance. But it was just another way of defining the church at the boundaries. Inside those boundaries the church was busily constructing young individuals who were learning to think of themselves as different, removed from the world.

The effect of this upon the soul is that we have lost something central to the definition of being human, namely, the ability to affirm the image of God in any other person. Without that we can only see those in other subcommunities as different from us. That makes them threatening, and that makes us a little less than human. So it will be without the recovery of substance to our pledge to live as a nation under God. That doesn't mean that my old home church should ever gain the power to make sure no one ever dances. It means that if we really want to live under God we can at least begin by affirming that God has more in mind for us than to be a collection of aliens who are wandering about trying to construct our own lives differently.

SOUL WEARY

Nomads don't speak much of living under God, or of heaven and hell, but that is only because they have abandoned the all-embracing connotations of it. Nevertheless, they search for heaven with great devotion, because even in the nomad the primal memory of paradise lingers, and they know they haven't found what they are looking for. They are desperately searching for home, where they will find an understanding of themselves that they can really believe. But typically they believe more in the search than in finding it. That is what drives all their movement and constant efforts at rearranging life.

As Dante expressed it, untethered lives are easily tossed about by the wind: "now here, then there, and up and down it drives them with never any hope to comfort them—hope not of rest but of suffering less." When he wrote those lines he was describing those in hell's circle for the lustful, "who make reason slave to appetite." The people the pilgrim met there had all been consumed by lust for their lovers, one even to the point of killing herself. But his description aptly describes the nomadic lust not just for sexual love, but for anything that is the next thing. Many of them are also killing themselves with desire for what is just beyond their grasp. Even if they do find a way to get hold of this desired object, it won't satisfy their yearning. They have to know that, but they choose to suppress such thoughts, making reason slave to appetite.

As a pastor who has spent many years caring for those being tossed about by the wind, I know that nomads don't enjoy being nomadic. It wears their souls down to float through one relationship, community, job, and philosophy of life after another.

When I met Ted he was thirty-one years old, divorced, the father of a little girl who lived with her mother, and new to our church. He had recently come to Washington to "get a fresh start" after his marriage fell apart. It didn't take him long to land a job with one of the high-tech firms in town, and it took even less time for him decide that he hated this job almost as much as the last one. But he had a lot of bills and child support to pay, so he really needed it. He had met a lot of people since moving to town, but he wasn't really close to anyone, including the woman from work with whom he sometimes spent the night. "At least," he sighed, "it keeps the loneliness away. You know the nights are the worst." After this extended introduction, I asked him why he had come to see me, thinking he would surely say that he was at the end of his rope and was wondering what God had to do with his life. Instead, he asked me if I could use my connections in the church to help him get a job on Capitol Hill.

When I hear these nomadic stories I am overwhelmed with compassion because the people who tell them are not evil, or even bad. But they're just as lost as they can be. Even they know that their real lust is only to get life right, if they could just find the right place. By the time they come to me they have made so many mistakes and hurt so many people, not to mention themselves, they just can't believe that there is enough grace to cover it all. Nor is it easy for me to convince them it can. Grace is all about what God does in our lives, but what they believe is that they are on their own. So they often respond to my counsel about receiving the good work of God with a polite smile and then ask me if I have any advice for something else they should try. Since the agenda of constructing their own lives has been so firmly inculcated, they just can't believe there is another way.

They have at their disposal more opportunities, freedom, resources, encouragement, and information than any generation ever to walk the face of the earth, but they still can't seem to make life work the way they want. That's because they belong to God, who reserves the sacred right to create a life.

In his treatise, "On the Incarnation," St. Athanasius claimed that our identity is directly derived from the God in whose image we were made. All of creation was created out of nothing, and thus even the dust of the ground that God used in forming humanity is derived from God. Turning away from God in the hope of finding a different source of identity, Athanasius warned, results not in becoming our own creations but in becoming nothing.[6] For we were created from nothing, and apart from God to nothing we return. This is exactly what we feel in our souls when we turn from God—nothing. Emptiness. And it is why we keep moving to the next thing in hopes of finding something that will again restore life to us.

This is what Blaise Pascal was warning future generations about with his famous prophecy: "We are never living, always hoping to live." Abraham Heschel referred to it as "A hesitation before birth." No one does this better than the nomads who constantly tell themselves that the next thing will satisfy their insatiable desire. But it never does. After obtaining the next thing, they soon discover it was only the birthplace of more desire. The psychiatrist Gerald May was expressing this same dynamic when he wrote, "There is a desire within each of us, in the deep center of ourselves that we call the heart. We are born with it, it is never completely satisfied, and it never dies. We are often unaware of it, but the desire is always awake."[7] Some believe that it is impossible for nomads to find relief because their desire only desires desire. But I think their desire desires home, which is possible to find, but they just can't quite believe it.

When the desire becomes too much, they can try to bury it beneath excessive work, another purchase, or another move to another place. They can try to numb the desire, but that will only lead to addiction. They can even spend most of life trying to tame the desire with respectability and the construction of a good reputation. But the wild desire just keeps breaking out of the closed chambers of the heart in unguarded moments. G. K. Chesterton has called this "the divine discontent" that incessantly reminds us we were created for something else. The nomads, for all of their meandering confusion, are at least clear that they haven't found what they are looking for. And so they continue to search for some glimpse of heaven.

At least the healthiest of the nomads continue their search. The danger is that at some point they will suffer too many disappointments and the burden of hoping in the next thing will become too great for their empty souls to bear. Then, in the words of Dante, they hope only for "suffering less." But when the nomad crosses that line, something inside begins to wither.

I have often wondered if this isn't what happened to my father, who died alone in the camping trailer somewhere in the middle of Florida. For so many years he drove that little trailer around and around in Dante's circle for the lustful. But after collecting so many disappointments in the things in which he searched for contentment, all of which came to him at great cost, he eventually stopped trying and aimlessly wandered around the country. He was then too afraid to try another relationship, job, or community because the hurt from his failures with past things was greater than his hope in the next thing. When that happened, all he wanted was to suffer less. That was probably what killed him.

In the leaf pocket of the tattered old notebook we found in his trailer, there was a note he had written to the last wife he left. I don't know if it was a copy of the letter he actually sent, or if this was the letter and it was never mailed. The letter apologizes for walking out on her one morning while she was still sleeping, and explains that he just didn't have the courage to call. The final sentence states, "Of all the bad things I have done you, the worst things I have done to myself." When a nomad makes that discovery he loses hope in his ability to find happiness. Despair is deadly to a nomadic soul, but is often where the search ends. In the words of Henri Frederic Amiel, "At bottom, everything depends upon the presence or absence of one single element in the soul—hope. All the activity of man, all his efforts and all his enterprises, presuppose a hope in him of attaining an end. Once kill this hope and his movements become senseless, spasmodic, and convulsive, like those of someone falling from a height."[8]

A Day of Small Things

One of the great indicators of lives that have fallen from the heights of magnificent, world-embracing hope is that they become "senseless, spasmodic, and convulsive" about things that have no eternal meaning. This was at the heart of the prophecy of Zechariah who warned the Hebrews when they were living in "a day of small things."[9] His stern judgment makes pressing claims against those today who worry only about whether they can afford the new SUV and still pay for the new bathroom, soccer camp, and having their teeth whitened. Then they worry that they will need a better job to afford all of these things, and that gets them worrying about how to make the next move. It is all that is left for them. There is simply no room in their hearts left to worry about things like the devastating scourge of AIDS that is killing millions in Africa. If forced to think about tragedies like that, nomads will say that they are glad to suffer less than these, and then add, "But I've got problems of my own." Eventually they find that not only can they not maintain hope for the pathos of the world, but they can't even maintain it for the small things that crowd their own lives.

No individual can maintain hope for long by conducting a solitary search for just my little place that is crammed full with my small things. The world has a way of crashing into any shelter we build for ourselves. It doesn't matter how beautiful the house is that you construct, or how high the walls are around your gated community, it is only a matter of time before all of the violence and heartache of the world comes for a visit.

Those who live in the pleasant outlying communities around Washington, D.C., encountered this recently when two men went on a fourteen-day shooting spree, killing people who thought they would suffer less if they were far from the violence of the inner-city streets. The terror that plagued those communities is known to every inner-city child, only they don't have any illusions about individual sanctuaries. If the sniper doesn't get you, then it is only a matter of time before cancer, a child in trouble, divorce, or the loss of a job does find its way to your home. I have been a pastor long enough to know that heartache can, and will, find every address. It will find the World Trade Towers, the Pentagon, the anthrax-infested government buildings, and certainly the cute little house tucked away in the 'burbs.

When I first arrived to serve as pastor of one of the congregations in Washington, I spent the better part of the first year asking the members what they most wanted from their church. I was surprised that the answer I heard more than all others was sanctuary. I understand that this felt need was born out of fatigue with living in a harsh city where one must constantly be on the defensive not only against violence but also the incessant conflict that is a part of a community devoted to the political process. So I spent the next ten years constantly trying to explain that the salvation offered by Jesus Christ isn't just one more futile means of finding protection for our own little dreams. To the contrary, it calls us to see that our hope is inextricably bound up with the hopes of the whole world.

As the incarnation of God, Christ was not simply offering us a personal salvation, a term the Bible never uses, but he was restoring the *axis mundi* that holds all of earth to the heaven from which it derives its life.

In his Sermon on the Mount, Jesus called us to live in the world with such a compassionate embrace that we can even love the enemy. He concluded that sermon by saying that if we live by his words our house will be built upon the rock, and it will withstand any of the prevailing storms of life. But to turn from Jesus' words, living anxiously for ourselves, is to build our house upon the sands. When the storms hit that house, he warned, "great will be its fall."[10] Since it is the world that scares or at least confuses us, we are tempted to run home for sanctuary from it. But only the home that is built with a vision for the salvation of the world will withstand its volatility, not to mention its evil.

LIVING BETWEEN PAST AND FUTURE

As Karl Barth claimed, the Christ who is for me is first and foremost the Christ who is for us. What he meant by that is not only that Jesus came to be the savior of the world, but in providing salvation to the individual, Christ reveals that an essential and defining element of the soul is its relationship to other souls. Thus, as Barth writes about the individual, "His conversion and renewal is not, therefore, an end in itself, as it has often been interpreted and represented in a far too egocentric Christianity. . . . When we convert and are renewed in the totality of our being, we cross the threshold of our private existence and move out into the open."[11] Home, the right place, is not a sanctuary from the world, but a place within the world where we go to understand our responsibility to it. And not just our responsibility to all people, but to all times. Home reminds us of the claims of both the past and future upon our lives.

Of course, none of us can build a home that is either theologically or compassionately big enough to make room for the whole world, the past, and the future. True, but we can inherit one, just as all of those who have gone before us. It was for this reason that Simone Weil claimed that "To be rooted is perhaps the most important and least recognized need of the human soul."[12] When we allow the story of our lives to be rooted in a story greater than ourselves, we are not limited to the small house that we can construct for ourselves.

In the church tradition of which I have been a part, it is typical for the worshipers to stand up and say the Apostles' Creed together. Every time I see the congregation doing that I am so struck by the countercultural nature of it all. There we are all essentially saying that some people who lived seventeen hundred years ago have written what we believe. If we were trying to be more relevant to the felt needs of the nomads who have wandered into church, this is the last thing we would do. Instead we would give everyone the opportunity to stand and tell us about the personal mission statements they wrote on their last retreat, or how they are doing with their self-actualization, or even about the personal doubts they have over the creed's doctrines. But making the church's tradition relevant to the small house of the individual is the last thing we want to do. The goal of our worship is to make the individual relevant to the great traditions of the church.

All week long, contemporary society saturates us with self. We have been taught to worry about my needs, my children, my money problems, my lack of fulfillment. Monday through Saturday it is all about me. So by the time I get to church on Sunday morning I am sick and tired of me. In the words of poet W. S. Merwin, "Send me out to another life Lord because this one is growing faint. I do not think it goes all the way."[13]

So I take my place in the larger community, stand with my little faith that leans on their great faith, and say the words: "I believe in God the Father Almighty, Maker of heaven and earth, and in Jesus Christ, his only Son our Lord, who was conceived by the Holy Ghost. . . ." Even if I don't fully believe or understand what I am saying, it doesn't really matter. It isn't my creed. It belongs to us. The creed belongs to martyrs who died for it, to the theologians who spent centuries hammering it out, to the children who were baptized under it, and to the holy community that has been guided by it for two thousand years. Why would I ever want to reduce that to me? Instead, what I need is to allow my life to get caught up in this much greater story about the Triune God who was at work long before I arrived for my little blip in history.

As I say that old creed, sing the old hymns, and place my life in front of an open Bible written so long ago, I hear again that the Holy Spirit has adopted me into the Son's beloved relationship with the Father. Then I remember my real home, where I am also called beloved. Having rehearsed this identity in worship, I can then return to my life with a clear vision of what is at its core. And I know I am so much more than a blip, because I have not only inherited a past identity but also a future hope. So I don't have to keep consuming things and time in the futile attempt to construct my own life. Now I am free to participate, in some way, in

God's great plans for the whole world. That's the gospel truth that can hold together heaven and earth, and even my meandering little life.

This isn't just my little faith talking. It is the great faith of the church that thrives in all places and at all times. And my place is in its midst.

TRAGIC IRONIES OF THE SOUL

So the path of the nomads, who are always searching for a heavenly home, passes through several painful ironies:

Living in a society that has tried to dismantle any connection between heaven and earth, they spend most of their life looking for a little heaven on earth.

Trying to construct their own lives, they give pieces of their soul to a plurality of competing interests that all seek to define them.

Insisting that relationships meet their needs, they sabotage authentic communion and suffer from loneliness.

Rejecting the exclusivity of a community defined at the center, they create small homogeneous communities defined at the borders.

Searching to find sanctuary from a confusing and fragmented world, they miss the *axis mundi* that holds the world together.

Seeking relevancy to their own life stories, they miss their opportunities to become relevant to a greater drama that could include them.

Constantly striving to change their own lives, they cannot be converted by the gospel.

There is another way. Rather than wasting our fleeting years wondering and wandering, we can just come home.

I am the way into the doleful city,
　　I am the way into eternal grief
　　I am the way to a forsaken race

Justice it was that moved my great creator
　　Divine omnipotence created me,
　　And mighty wisdom joined with primal love

Before me nothing but eternal things
　　Were made and I shall last eternally
　　Abandon every hope, all who enter

I saw these words spelled out in somber colors
　　inscribed along the edge above the gate;
　　"Master," I said, "these words are cruel." . . .

"My son," the gentle master said to me,
　　"all those who perish in the wrath of God
　　assemble here from all parts of the earth;

they want to cross the river, they are eager;
　　it is Divine Justice that spurs them on,
　　turning the fear they have into desire.

Dante, *The Inferno,* III. 1–12, 121–26, pp. 89, 93

$$5$$

Beginning the Journey Home

Going Down to Go Up

After over twenty years of watching human souls as a pastor, I have become convinced that our greatest fear is that we're stuck with ourselves. That's why we are constantly trying to change our lives to become different, and ironically, the relentlessness of our own efforts is what gets us lost, preventing us from being changed by God.

God doesn't have any interest in changing us into different people. His idea of salvation is to convert us into being who we were created to be from the beginning. That is why he is calling us home, because only there is our true identity clear. But the road home always passes through hell.

WAKING UP

The journey home is not easier than the one that simply meanders through life; in some ways it's so much harder, but it does lead to our salvation. Perhaps the hardest part of the trip is the beginning, where we must confess that we are lost. We are ready to tell the truth about that not when we have learned salvation formulas to which we give intellectual assent, but when we discover that like Dante we have awakened to find ourselves in a dark wood because we have somehow wandered off from the straight path.

The great and hopeful turn in life, the turn that transforms people from meandering nomads into hopeful pilgrims, begins with the confession that they are lost. Only then can they make use of the means of grace God provides to begin their pilgrimage home. But as long as they continue to think they can manage their way out of the dark wood, they'll only wander deeper into it.

It was the alcoholics of our congregation that taught me this. They've learned that it is never possible to help alcoholics with recovery as long as they are functioning alcoholics. "So how do I help them?" I asked the Alcoholics Anonymous group that meets in the basement of our church. "Pray that they hit bottom soon," they told me. "There is nothing else to do." It is certainly possible to try interventions, but that is only a way of shaking someone. It's still up to the addict to wake up, and that won't happen until he or she realizes that the days of functioning have come to an end and it's time to confess the need for help.

If there is any grace in being addicted to booze, drugs, gambling, or sex, it is that these are not socially approved vices. So there are a variety of social structures that try to mitigate against addiction to these things, and lots of treatment centers to help these addicts turn from their self-destruction. But those who are addicted to the socially approved vices of power, money, and self-improvement have a harder time realizing that the better they function with these addictions the more lost they become. There are no recovery hospitals for those addicted to greed or control. That's because society approves of these addictions and perceives them as the means of changing life and becoming different, which is one of our great national illusions. As with the disapproved alcoholics, as long as the approved addicts function well they will only grow more addicted to the things that are actually destroying them, and more sleepy to the reality of their predicament. In time they will even prefer the sleepiness because then they can't feel the pain from all the disappointments of life. So they just keep consuming more money and power. Again, one can try to intervene, and as a pastor I have tried this plenty, but I know it is still up to the addict to wake up. Usually this realization occurs at the bottom of a dark wood of tragedy that was caused by walking through life asleep. A spouse walks out, a child acts out, or a company throws them out. And if they are blessed, they wake up.

Dante spent much of his life trying to rise to a position of great power in his beloved city of Florence. Early on he would have claimed that he was only trying to serve the city, but as is often the case with politicians, he soon found that he was serving politics itself. Before long he had became entangled in the battles between the Black and White Guelfs, the competing political allegiances of his day. When the pope intervened in the struggle with political agendas of his own, Dante found himself exiled, under a sentence of execution if he ever returned to Florence. That was about the time he woke up.

For a short while he flirted with the idea of organizing a comeback with some of the other exiles, but as a man who had truly lifted his eyes to the reality of his life, he knew now that his real yearning wasn't to get back to Florence but to his real home. The one he could never lose. To find that home he needed not to become more powerful, but to confess his powerlessness.

Going Down to Go Up

In *The Inferno,* after the pilgrim wakes ups in the dark wood, he sees the mountain of purgatory standing before him. Later, this mountain will be explored further, but for now it is sufficient to say that it represents the hard journey up to our home. Actually, it is so hard that it can only be ascended by the grace of God, which comes every step of the way. At first, the pilgrim is delighted to finally discover this path to his true home and so he quickly rushes to the gate. But when he arrives there he finds the entrance blocked by ferocious animals who represent the debased, beastly creature he has become.

Upon discovering that his sin is preventing him from just walking home, he is inconsolable, which is an early sign of true confession. He realizes the desperation of his condition as a wolf "racked with every kind of greediness" forces him to retreat "back to where the sun is mute."[1] It is at this point in the journey that he meets Virgil, who has been sent from heaven to be his rational guide through much of the journey home.[2] When the pilgrim sees Virgil, he cries out for salvation from the terrifying animals he fears will devour him, confessing that he will be destroyed by his own animal nature.

Virgil responds to the tears of the pilgrim by promising that the beasts will not consume him, and he reminds him of the splendors of the heaven where his journey will end. "But," the guide explains, "you must journey down another road . . . if you ever hope to leave this wilderness."[3] In other words, we have to go down to go up, because no one just climbs home to God. The path begins at the gate of hell.

In order to see the light of heaven that shines into the dark wood, we must confront what is at the core of our sin. This confession opens up a place in our tightly constructed lives that allows the light of forgiveness to shine in. Seeing that hope, we then have the opportunity to repent, or turn, and follow the path of grace all the way home. But none of that happens without the hard work of confessing sin, which is another old doctrine that is hard for the nomad to grasp.

The biblical understanding of sin is deeper than just the failures we commit and the lies we tell. At its essence, sin is separation from God. Having chosen to turn to another source of life other than God, we have separated ourselves from him. Along the way on our separate journey we will tell all sorts of lies, not the least of which is that we can live apart from God. And we traveled so far in the wrong direction that it takes a while to get back home. In the words of Karl Barth again, "We cannot say—for it simply would not be true—that we see in the Bible converted men. What we can and must say is that we see men caught up in the movement of conversion. . . . They had moved away from God. And it is claiming too much to say that they moved right back to God. But what we must say is that they can no longer proceed without God. On the contrary they are compelled to rise up and come to Him, and are now in the process of doing so. This is the movement of conversion."[4]

Even the first steps of this movement are terrifying. So much so that it feels like we are descending into hell, the ultimate place of separation. That is exactly where the rational guide leads us—not because we have to stay there, but because it only makes sense that we have to confess and confront the truth about all we have done to break communion with God before we're ready to hear the greater truth about the grace that forgives and carries us home.

When we confess, we do not just list our most recent sins, but we confess our sinful nature. We tell the truth that we sin because we are good at it, it is what we know, and we are hopelessly addicted to it. That is what the sign above the gate to hell is trying to tell us when it says,

"Abandon every hope all who enter." To confess is to admit the hopelessness of our situation. Hell is where we have descended when we realize we will never manage our way out of the dark wood, for the only way we have been able to manage sin is with more sin. Now we realize we are stuck with ourselves, which is our greatest fear, our hell, and we have abandoned all hope.

It is significant that Virgil was sent from heaven before the pilgrim began his frightening journey down into the hell of confession. What this means is that grace precedes confession, guides it, and makes the movement possible. The historical reality of what Christ did on the cross means that we confess our sins because God has already forgiven us. That is our only hope, the one we were not counting on, and the one that appears only after we abandoned all others. So we do not confess in order to receive grace, but in order to enjoy it. If confession preceded grace, it would mean we deserve God's mercy by our contrition. What we deserve is the last thing we want, and a little stroll through hell will make that all too clear.

As Dante will illustrate, it is only by climbing down to the lowest circle of hell that we can turn up and begin the climb up to God. Only when we arrive at the bottom of our sinful nature, confronting how far it has separated us from God, are we ready for repentance, which means to make a change and turn our lives in a different direction. One of the most common mistakes I have witnessed in the members of our church, as well as my own life, is to begin the process of repentance too soon. We may tell ourselves that we are at the bottom of our confession, but that is only because we are afraid to travel deeper. We'll know when we are the bottom of hell because, as Dante discovered, the journey itself has then turned up allowing us to see the first glimmers of heaven's light.

Another poet, John Donne, writing several hundred years after Dante, expressed this same dynamic in confession in his poem "A Hymn to God the Father":

> Wilt thou forgive that sin where I begun,
>   Which was my sin, though it were done before?
> Wilt thou that sin through which I run,
>   And do run still, though still I do deplore?
>   When thou hast done, thou hast not done,
>   For I have more.

> Wilt thou forgive that which I have won
>> Others to sin, and made my sin their door?
> Wilt thou forgive that sin which I did shun
>> A year or two, but wallow'd in a score?
>>> When thou hast done, thou hast not done,
>>> For I have more.

> I have a sin of fear, that when I have spun
>> My last thread, I shall perish on the shore;
> But swear by thyself, that at my death thy Son
>> Shall shine as he shines now, and heretofore;
>>> And, having done that, thou hast done;
>>> I fear no more.[5]

Using a play on his own name, Donne makes the point that the Father "hast not done" simply through the act of human confession, which really never ends. But eventually, through the process of telling the hard truth, we are drawn to the forgiving grace of Jesus Christ on the cross. As that grace shines into the hell into which we have descended, we fear no more because we can now see that, in Christ, salvation is completed. Now with Donne we can say, "thou hast done," just as thou hast you and me.

THE DESCENT INTO CONFESSION

Before joining the pilgrim Dante on his journey down into hell, it is important to remember that *The Inferno* was never meant to be his speculation about what the real place called hell is all about. The images depicted in all of the books of *The Divine Comedy* are meant to help us understand how to live our earthly lives in the light of their eternal significance. He wants us to know how to live not as lost nomads, but as pilgrims who have begun the journey home.

For example, according to *The Inferno*, hell is organized into nine descending concentric circles. Upper hell consists of the first five circles, which are reserved for those who have lived lives of "incontinence," by which he means without discipline. Here we encounter souls that were depleted by the first of the five deadly sins: lust, gluttony, avarice, sloth, and wrath. Lower hell consists of the next four circles, where we meet the sins of violence. This includes the remaining two deadly sins of envy and pride, which are spread out over those four circles. His point in this architecture is to explain, "how incontinence offends God the least, and merits the least blame."[6] By contrast, we have built a society that worries more about the sins of the flesh than the sins of the soul. We punish severely those who have committed sins of lust and sloth but admire those whose envy and pride has allowed them to accomplish and accumulate so much, even though this does violence to the poor of the earth. But from the perspective of heaven, our sins are weighted differently.

Rather than tracing the pilgrim's steps through each circle of hell, more help is gained by examining several of the insights that Dante makes along the way about what has happened to our souls in the hell of our own creation.

Hell Is the Place Where Your Soul Is Consumed by Your Vice

The punishments Dante encounters in the inferno depict the souls of sinners who are wrapped around their vices to the exclusion of everything else. Again, that's because Dante thought of sin the way we think of addiction. It is a way of losing the whole by being preoccupied with the particular. That is hell. It is what separates us from our home with the God who created us to enjoy the whole garden. But as Adam and Eve discovered, it is when we become obsessed with one piece of forbidden fruit that we lose paradise. Usually it is only then that we realize it was paradise. Then it is only the longing for paradise that remains, which ironically means that we are actually longing to be more than the embodiment of our desire.

The old pietists used to use a term called "a besetting sin." Your besetting sin is the one to which you are most addicted, and the one that is most tempting. Different people have different besetting sins, but we all have at least one. The first car I owned as a young man had a terrible alignment problem, which made the front wheels always want to veer into the ditch. Being too broke to have the problem fixed, I just drove the car by always pulling on the steering wheel to keep the car moving straight. That is how one must respond to their particular besetting sin. You have to constantly and consciously pull your life in the opposite direction from the temptation, or it will end up in the ditch.

The people we meet in hell have become so consumed by their besetting sins that not only are they in the ditch but they have actually become their sin. Dante presents real people in hell who had actually created their own hell before they died. But in the inferno their lives lose all of their subtlety and veneer and they are seen simply from the raw perspective of their souls.

Alessio Interminei, who became a political success in Florence through flattery, now finds that his mouth fills with excrement every time he opens it.[7]

The lovers, Francesca and Paolo, who were killed by her jealous husband who caught them in bed, are now stuck holding each other for eternity. As Francesca says, "Love, that excuses no one from loving, seized me so strongly with delight in him that as you see he never leaves my side."[8] They gave themselves over to the lust that both literally and metaphorically took away their lives, and now they cannot escape each other.

The wrathful, whom we meet in the fourth circle, spend eternity tearing each other apart. When the pilgrim tries to recognize anyone there, Virgil tells him, "Yours is an empty hope: their undistinguished life that made them foul now makes it harder to distinguish them. Eternally the two will come to blows; then from the tomb they will be resurrected: these with tight fists, those without any hair. It was squandering and hoarding that robbed them of the lovely world, and got them in this brawl."[9]

The suicides in a lower rung of hell are forced to spend eternity dragging around their bodies because they did not want to live in the life they were given. As one of them tells him, "I turned my home into my hanging place."[10] The reason they are placed in lower hell is not because they were so desperate, but because they gave up on home. This is not to say there is no redemption for suicide, although as a medieval Catholic Dante would have his doubts, but it is to claim that the last thing you want to do is self-destruct on the search for home.

All of the souls in hell are the embodiment of desperation, and all of them have self-destructed by succumbing to their besetting sin. None of them had to do that. All of them took a blessed gift from God and distorted it into their god, and people always end up looking like the idols they serve. This is the temptation nomads face when they think of the world less as the blessed garden to be cared for and more as the wide expanse of opportunities to be explored. By refusing to settle down, they can avoid responsibility for any particular part of the world. This inevitably distorts the next place into an idol that promises freedom from responsibility but at the cost of reducing the soul to its insatiable yearning. The next place wasn't created to be the answer to the yearning, only as another place to be of service along the way in coming home.

Warning us about the possibility of distorting a blessing into an idol, Jesus told us in the Sermon on the Mount, "If your right eye offends you, tear it out. . . . If your right hand causes you to sin, cut it off and throw it away; it is better for you to lose one of your members than to have the whole body and be thrown into hell."[11] Jesus did not mean for us to take that literally. He meant what he meant—don't be consumed by something that was given as a blessing. The blessing is just a care package from home. The point of it is to make us thankful, and maybe a little homesick.

Hell Is Being Unable to See the Present

At one point on the journey, the pilgrim comes across a heretic who asks if his son is still alive. The pilgrim is confused by this question, since those in hell have perfectly clear vision about the past and future. The past they see as that which has defined them, and the future they know because it is determined by the past. But no one in hell has any idea what is happening in the present. The damned man tries to explain this to the pilgrim. "'Down here we see like those with faulty vision who only see,' he said, 'what's at a distance; this much the sovereign Lord grants us here. When events are close to us, or when they happen our mind is blank.'"[12]

It is ironic, again, that this particular heretic was an Epicurean who during his days on earth exalted in the pleasures of the present day and denied the existence of an afterlife. Now all he has is the afterlife and his painful memories of a wasted life, but neither the pleasures of the day or even an ability to know what day it is.

Whenever people turn their attention away from the future, they say things like, "Let's just enjoy the day we have." But that is precisely what cannot be done without living in all three tenses of past, present, and future. The day we have is never understood, and certainly not appreciated, on its own terms. It always exists as part of a greater whole. Cut off from the past and future, the present can never be seen for all of the meaning it holds.

Postmodern novelists write about nomadic characters who simply wander from one experience and relationship to another. Typical of these is Richard Ford, who claims, "All we really want is to get to the place where the past can explain nothing about us, and we can get on with life."[13] That is because the past makes claims about our identity, and the reason nomads wander around is to escape that very identity. But none of them ever succeed, because the identity of the past isn't inculcated only in a particular community, but also in the longing of the human heart for meaning. And the heart travels with the nomad. Having cut themselves off from that past, however, nomads have a hard time finding meaning either to their own lives or the chaotic world around them. As Ford confesses, "My characters generally embody the attitude that life is always going to be a damn nasty and probably baffling business, but someone has to go on slogging through it."[14] There it is—all that's left when we live only in the nasty, baffling day we have.

Perhaps the most telling way that contemporary nomads attempt to live only in the present is through the accumulation of so much debt. In giving us houses that now rival the delights of the Epicureans and the luxury of the Roman Caesars, society distracts us from ever finding home. At a time when families are smaller than ever, the nomads are buying larger houses, which means they also have to buy more furniture to fill them, and that means they have to earn more and more money to pay their debt. Before long, they are again having to hit the road in search of a better paying job. When they find that better paycheck, the first thing they do is buy an even bigger house, and the cycle starts again. It isn't only their future they are mortgaging, but also their souls. They think that if they could just accumulate enough they would have a home. But a home is never a place that exists only in the present tense. It has a past that is filled with memories, and offers to keep its inhabitants safely into the future. Without that, all the nomad has is a big house, a lot of furniture, and more debt than can ever be repaid. Since the nomad knows this is not home, he or she so easily abandons this house for another one.

By looking to society to provide more and more consumer goods, the nomads have allowed themselves to be reduced to consumers who can never quite get enough. The only counsel the marketers of these goods offer is to become a good consumer who has a right to a good deal. In the 1950s, we were dangerously close to turning corporations into idols that we would serve. By way of reaction, in the sixties and seventies, we denounced these same icons as oppressors. But since the affluent era of the eighties, we have come to think of these same corporations not only as resources for our accumulation but also as sponsors of our entertainment. It is hard to attend a sporting event without entering an arena that bears the name of a large corporation, or to watch more than five minutes of television without hearing, "brought to you by . . ." Even our clothes bear the insignia of corporations, reducing us to walking billboards. We might as well get tattoos for our foreheads that just say CONSUMER. It would be a more relevant mark of the beast upon a people who are trying to distract themselves through the day they have, which is now the primary function of all our consumption.

Again the terrible ironies of the alienated nomadic soul become evident. By trying to focus only on the comforts and entertainments of the present, we cannot see the present for what it really is. The past does not fill it with meaning and identity. The future does not break into the hard realities of the day with hope and direction. So all that is left is, well, just another day. And that is hell.

People Are in Hell Because They Want to Be

When we accompany the pilgrim on his frightening journey down the circles of hell, it is clear that nobody is having a very good time, but neither is anyone denying that they belong there. They all know that this is the poetic fulfillment of their lives, and since after death no one can pretend anymore, they know this place of separation from grace is where they belong. To be disgraced means to be removed (dis) from the means of grace. To spend one's days on earth constantly doing everything possible to live without the grace of God is to live disgracefully. So why would anyone who lived life that way want to turn to grace after death? After passing the river of death people don't become different. As Dante claims, they just become a truer form of themselves.

The sign above the gate to hell begins with three "I am" statements. "I am the way into the doleful city. I am the way to eternal grief. I am the way to a forsaken race." For Dante, these are inversions of the christological statements made by Jesus who claimed, "I am the gate. Whoever enters by me will be saved."[15] Hell exists as the inversion of the means of salvation. It is the eternal image of making one's home in a place that can never be home, because it has no savior and thus no bestowal of grace.

The second stanza of the sign above the gate claims, "Justice it was that moved my great Creator. Divine omnipotence created me, and highest wisdom joined with primal love." Isn't that striking? We tend to think of hell only as a place of eternal punishment where an angry God sends sinners. But Dante is claiming that from the beginning even hell was created as an act of love, because God is only giving people what they want.

When as a pastor I talk with the nomads who are burning through so many relationships, jobs, and experiences, and yet still thirst for the next thing, it occurs to me that they have to know that the next thing isn't going to make them any happier than the other things have. But wanting is a bad narcotic. The more of it you take in, the more it starts to ruin your life, until your fleeting years are wasted with insatiable cravings.

Contemporary culture encourages this addiction. Daily, hundreds of advertisements pass by our eyes, and none of them are simply marketing products to give us what we want. Instead they are telling us what we not only want but need. Before we know we have been sold on this need. It is then a small step to think we also need a better job, a nicer lifestyle, and a more promising future. But the need is never fully satisfied. That's the way addictions work. The more of the narcotic you get, the more you need, which means you are never satisfied.

When I speak with those struggling with the narcotic of more, they may be choosing to ignore the realization, but I think they know they are addicted. It doesn't matter. Insight means nothing to an addict. They cannot help but devote themselves to the next thing, even though they know it will not satisfy them either. They have grown so accustomed to disappointment that they would be disappointed without it.

"What would you do," I have sometimes asked, "if this next job really made you happy?" The answer is always the same. "Well, I don't know." Right. But I know what they would do. It would not be long before they sabotaged the contentment because they only trust feelings of discontentment and craving. They may sing and lament, "I can't get no satisfaction," but that is largely because they just can't handle it.

Early in his journey through hell, the pilgrim was dismayed to find so many people damned to this eternal future. But Virgil reassures him saying, "they want to cross the river, they are eager; it is divine justice that spurs them on, turning the fear they have into desire."[16] People choose eternity in hell for the same reason they created hell on earth—

because they prefer the misery they know to the mystery they do not. Why are angry people angry, hurt people hurt, and addicts addicted? It isn't because they are unaware of the possibilities of redemption. It is because they have befriended their pain and trust it only. To benefit from a savior, you have to trust him instead, which is what we call faith. Hell is the place where there is faith in nothing but heartache.

Hell Is Where You Are Stuck with Yourself without the Possibility of Redemption

Dante is very careful to make the point that hell isn't the place where all sinners go. There are also sinners in purgatory and even paradise. Nor is hell distinguished as the place where those are sent who do not confess their sins. Everyone in hell is very good about confessing the truth of their lives, and many of them had made these confessions during their time on earth.

The distinctive thing about those in hell has to do with repentance. They never turned to the Savior, but turned instead to themselves. Only they didn't turn to the true self created by God. Rather, they turned to a more desired image of themselves. But they never really changed; they just got lost in a dream that had become a nightmare. Before long the only way they know to get out of the nightmare is to try again to change, which won't work any better than the last effort. The more the disappointments pile up, the more they fear they will never get out of this nightmare of being stuck with themselves. It never occurs to them to simply wake up to the futility of these efforts, and that's why hell is a hopeless place.

I see nomads living in this self-created hell all of the time. Most people who make appointments to see their pastor aren't really addicted to the marketing strategies of advertisers. By the time they come to me, they are not looking just to lose a few pounds or shed a few wrinkles. What they want is a completely different life. It reminds me sometimes of playing Scrabble—when you can't do anything with the letters you've got, you're allowed to use a turn to just dump them all and draw new, more promising letters. That's what nomads eventually want. They want to toss all of the pieces of life back in the box in the hopes of getting something else with which to create joy. And that is why they so readily move, seeking not just a different town but the opportunity to be a different person. They may say that they hope the next job or relationship will give them the chance to finally be themselves, but I have learned that what they are really hoping is to become someone other than themselves.

The reason they long for a different life is because the last message a nomadic society is going to tell them is that they shouldn't change. Everything around them is changing, and in hundreds of ways they hear they must keep changing as well. Change implies a judgment on the way things were, and this judgment cannot help but make its way into the human soul.

The problem is that we aren't really good at making minor changes to our lives, and we have no idea how to create a different life. We have tried all of the self-help books and videos. We've tried going back to graduate school, Weight Watchers, pottery classes, yoga, and the new health club. It doesn't really matter what self-improvement program we wander into, it is still just the same person who keeps showing up in the mirror every morning. That's because these are all just ways of turning back to ourselves in hopes of finding a way to be different.

The Bible doesn't offer us an ounce of help in becoming different. Instead, it calls us to conversion. But this is never a conversion into being a different person. Rather, it is only a way of being converted back to being who we were created to be in the beginning. God created us as humans with particularly unique forms, shapes, and personalities. Then he called his creation good. So the last thing we want to be praying for is to be something other than what God had in mind. It is only a way of criticizing the good creation of God by saying, "Not good enough." That is the height of arrogance born out of a sense of pride, and it ends in the lowest circle of hell. This is not to say that our humanity does not need to be redeemed, but the redemption we are offered by God results only in becoming a purer form of ourselves.

As a pastor, I find that many people have grave doubts about that. One of the reasons some come to church is precisely because they think God doesn't like them any more than they like themselves, and surely he has a plan to change them into somebody else. They don't like themselves because they have been taught not to. The lessons began at an early age and continue to the end of life. When they were children, they were judged inadequate by their parents, and when they became parents they were judged inadequate by their children. Every day they encounter more judgments that claim they are not smart enough, pretty enough, or successful enough. So they tell themselves, "God can just take a number and join the long line of those who want me to be different."

These suspicions about God's displeasure are only fueled by all of the rhetoric they have heard from the many preachers who beat them on the head and shoulders with fear about God's judgment. One of the reasons why judgmental forms of religion are flourishing in our country is because so many people think the angry preacher is right. The message certainly resonates with everything else they've heard about themselves from society. Thus, in spite of all the culture bashing these preachers do, they are just one more voice of culture telling people to be different.

The Bible speaks clearly about our need to confess sin, accept forgiveness, and repent or turn our lives around. But when we make this turn under the guidance and power of the Holy Spirit, we find that we are now moving back in the direction of home, where we can only be who we have really been all along. This means that the sin from which we most need to repent is pretending to be someone different for so many long and wasted years. We really aren't angry, cynical, greedy, or frightened victims. We may have been acting like that, but God didn't make us that way. And when we receive the forgiveness accomplished by the death of Christ upon the cross it was not just so we could now be angry or frightened Christians. It was so we could be free from the power of the pretense and the enslaving illusion that the next change will really work, to now enjoy God's good creation of our lives.

While vacationing recently in Florence, Italy, I had the opportunity to visit some of the finest art museums in the world. As I walked through them I was struck by how many of the pre-Renaissance paintings portrayed the anger of God. The scenes were dark, the themes were frequently of judgment, and the people were diminished, dour, and two-dimensional. In the middle of this trip, during my morning devotions, I came upon Psalm 149:4 that claims, "The Lord takes pleasure in his people." On that same day I began to observe the works of Michelangelo, who had apparently also stumbled across this same verse. The tourists, I noticed, tended to hustle by the medieval art as quickly as possible, but when they got to the statue of David, everyone wanted only to stand there and gaze upon such beauty.

What were we staring at? At a depiction of humanity as it was created to be, at "a man after God's own heart," and at a glimpse of life from an artist who believed God is pleased with what he created. As everyone knows, the image was already in the stone. Michelangelo was just freeing it by removing everything that didn't belong there. That is what redemption looks like. And to wander through life trapped in the hopes of being different, well, that looks like hell.

At the Center of Hell Is a Distorted Vision of God

When Virgil and the pilgrim finally make it down to the bottom of hell, they find the giant Lucifer, with three heads. From the chest down he is frozen in ice. Because he betrayed God, he is joined in this last circle by all the other traitors of earth. With each of his three heads Lucifer is eating the three men that Dante considers the greatest traitors of all time: Judas, Brutus, and Cassius, which signifies the betrayal of both the spiritual and political kingdoms.

When the pilgrim sees this giant, he says, "If once he was as fair as now he's foul and dared to raise his brow against his Maker, it is fitting that all grief should spring from him."[17] All of our grief, Dante claims, springs from betrayal, of which Lucifer is the embodiment. By giving him three heads the poet is telling us that the devil exists as a distortion of the Trinity. We also betray the Creator when we see him not as he is revealed in Jesus Christ, but with a distorted vision of him. And any distorted vision of God springs from the giant distortion, Lucifer.

When my parishioners talk to me about the problems they are having living as Christians, I usually find that at the bottom of these problems is a related problem in their image of God. Those who are judgmental or angry have been worshiping an angry, judgmental God who is never satisfied. Those who cannot give themselves to love really have doubts that God has given himself to them in the passion of Jesus Christ. Anyone who cannot live with joy cannot believe that God loves to laugh. (But why else would he have created ostriches?) This means that the way we get rid of the things about ourselves that we really don't like is not by trying hard, and certainly not by looking at other creatures that we prefer to ourselves, but by looking at God through the lens of Scripture. Until our image of God is redeemed, we will never succeed in appropriating redemption for ourselves, because creatures always look like the god they worship.

Satan is never more devilish than when he is perverting our vision of God. That is why preachers have to talk not only about the human predicament but even more about the nature of God as revealed in Christ and made known to us through the work of the Holy Spirit. When that Spirit is inspiring our understanding of the Triune God, we see him not through the distorting lense of our fathers, teachers, or bosses, for whom we were never quite good enough, but as the Savior who was dying to love us. Being good enough is really quite beside the point. Not only does the Spirit convince us of this grace, it also transforms us into the very image of the Son, from one degree of glory to the next, until we begin to look like the Beloved, in whom we live and have our being. This is what it means to "be" in Christ.

This transformation happens not in a moment, but as professor Barth said, as a movement of conversion. The reason Lucifer was depicted in ice, and not in flames as we typically think, is because Dante wanted to stress how a distorted vision of God prevents us from making this converting and sanctifying movement. The way we get stuck on the pilgrimage home, where we are finally fully able to be all that we were created to be, is by thinking of God as something less than he has revealed himself to be.

There is nothing worse to a pilgrim than being stuck. There is also nothing worse to a nomad, but ironically, nomads are stuck in thinking that if they just keep moving they can change themselves into being a more cherished image of themselves. But that is only one more distortion of God. We are made in his image, and we will never make it home to him by pretending to belong to any other image maker, least of all the one we dream up for ourselves. That is just one more distortion of God from which we must repent and turn in order to find our way out of the hell we have created for ourselves.

So the pilgrim and Virgil had to climb down the giant to get to the bottom of the great distortion. At that very moment they discovered that the journey was finally turning up. This is when we are done with confession, and when true repentance becomes possible—when we arrive at the bottom of our perverted image of God.

> We climbed, he first and I behind, until
> through a small round opening ahead of us
> I saw the lovely things the heavens hold,
>
> And we came out to see once more the stars.[18]

We made our way along that lonely plain
     like men who seek the right path they have lost,
     counting each step a loss till it is found.

When we had reached a place where the cool shade
     allowed the dew to linger on the slope,
     resisting a while longer the sun's rays,

my master placed both of his widespread hands
     gently upon the tender grass, and I,
     who understood what his intention was,

offered my tear-stained face to him, and he
     made my face clean, restoring its true color,
     once buried underneath the dirt of Hell.[1]

                    Dante, *Purgatory*, I. 118–29, p. 4

6

The Memory of the Father's House
The Great Turnaround

I am always dismayed to find people who do the hard work of confessing the truth of how lost they've become, maybe even getting to the bottom of it, but they stop there and never head for home. They're stuck in hell. No sin is greater than being too proud to come home once grace has made a way. That is why the lowest circle of the inferno is filled with hubris.

If confession is the hardest part of the journey home, perhaps the most crucial is the turn out of confession into repentance. This turn begins simply with a memory of the gracious Father's house, which is also when our true identity begins to return.

CRIPPLING GUILT

One of the questions I keep asking the wonderful therapists I have known is how people move from discovering insights to making changes in their lives. Just because their clients gain insights on why they do what they don't want to do, that doesn't prevent them from continuing to do it. They can understand all their family-of-origin issues and still be addicted to them. One of the questions the therapists keep asking me is, How do we use theological language to effect existential healing? Just because people make it through the prayer of confession with integrity, that doesn't mean that they are walking out of the church worship service as new creations.

I think the answer to both of our questions is that change, or turning, begins with accepting forgiveness. It isn't something we do, for part of what we were confessing in the frozen lake at the bottom of hell is that we are helpless and immobilized by our sin. Change begins as something we allow forgiving grace to do within us.

According to New Testament Greek, to be forgiven means to be freed. The same word can even be translated either way. This means that God's forgiveness of our sins does so much more than declaring us off the hook for our transgressions. Instead, it proclaims that we are free from the frozen immobility that sin causes in a life. Only then can we continue on in the journey toward home, where we are changed back into the beloved identity of being the sons and daughters of God.

Once, when asked to heal a paralyzed man, Jesus responded by saying, "Son, your sins are forgiven . . . stand up, take your mat and go to your home."[2] When some of the Jewish scribes standing nearby heard this they began to wonder why Jesus healed the man by declaring that his sins were forgiven. So do we. There are other places in the Scriptures that indicate infirmity is not caused by sin. Job didn't sin. And Jesus didn't usually heal by pronouncing absolution. So why does he do so here? Because he's making a point.

His point is that we are crippled by our guilt more than anything else. We have guilt because of what we have done and what we have left undone. We have guilt because we got worried, tried to take over for God, and made a bigger mess than the thing we were worried about. And we have guilt because we violated the holy laws that graciously provided us a means of loving God and living a life we could enjoy.

We don't actually break God's laws. They are still standing whether we obey them or not. To try to break God's law would be like trying to break the law of gravity. If you try it, you'll discover the law always wins. But when we violate God's law, it breaks us. That is what guilt and shame is all about. Until we know we are forgiven, we will never walk again. We will certainly never make it home.

"Which is easier to say?" Jesus asked the scribes. "'Your sins are forgiven,' or to say, 'Stand up, take your mat and walk?'" It is as if Jesus is saying, "Look we can talk about healing if you want. Or we can talk about the psychologically complex explanations for guilt. We can talk about Freud's social constraints, Jung's dark shadow, or Maslow's self-actualization. We can talk about wholeness, self-esteem, victimization, and the other things that aren't offensive to anyone. But at some point somebody has to start talking about forgiveness, because it is the only way to get rid of guilt."

Guilt is the great universal disease of the soul. We have all infected ourselves with it, even those protesting religious leaders who were repressing their guilt with moralisms. Guilt is the hardest disease of all to heal. Hearing that you are forgiven is the only antidote.

This means that the thing we need most from others is the declaration that in Jesus Christ we are forgiven. There are so many things we can do for ourselves in the spiritual life. We can read the Bible, pray, serve, and even worship. But when it comes to hearing that we are forgiven, we all need a faithful priest to speak the words to us. The point of the Protestant Reformation was not to do away with the priesthood, but to turn all believers into priests who can offer absolution.

When you have finally found the courage to tell someone the truth about your guilt, the last thing you want to hear is that you're not so bad. What you want to hear, what you have to hear, is that you are forgiven. It's the only way you are going to get back on your feet.

After hearing that you are forgiven, the only thing that follows is to stand up, turn, and get moving again. In the words of St. Augustine, "You have been a paralytic inwardly. You did not take charge of your bed. Your bed took charge of you."[3] Or in the words of Jesus Christ, "I say to you, stand up, take your mat and go to your home."

WALKING IN FREEDOM

Not only do we have to hear the declaration that we are forgiven, we have to believe it, or we will never find freedom from the paralysis created by our guilt.

Writing to the Romans, Paul said, "Do not be conformed to this world, but be transformed by the renewal of your minds, so that you may discern what is the will of God—what is good, and acceptable, and perfect."[4] The verb *conformed* in the Greek is in the middle voice, which means it is something that we do to ourselves. By contrast, the verb *transformed* is in the passive voice, meaning it is something that happens to us. So Paul is telling the church to stop forcing themselves into the mold for their lives. It has only immobilized you in sin, which keeps your soul alienated from God. Instead, he says, allow yourselves to be transformed by setting your mind on God's will for you. That will is that you may discern what is good, acceptable, and perfect—which you'll never do if you stop at the realization that you are a sinner. That is not God's will for you.

God's will was revealed in creation when he called you good, and in the redemption made possible in the death and resurrection of Jesus Christ, and in the sanctifying power of the Holy Spirit who engrafts you into the life of the Son. In his letters to the New Testament churches, Paul writes at length about our calling to live in Christ, by which he means accepting our identity as the adopted and beloved children of God, who are no longer aliens but at home with the true Holy Family of Father, Son, and Spirit. So, look at Jesus Christ, because that is who you really are as the child of God. "And if children, then heirs, heirs of God, and joint heirs with Jesus Christ."[5] That's who you are. But you will never be yourself until you walk away from the old alienated condition. And you will never be able to walk away from that until you set your mind not on your confessed sin, but on the transforming freedom offered in being forgiven.

Down through the history of the church, our theologians have debated exactly how Christ atones for our alienating sin and frees us to be reunited with God. Everyone in the debate is able to quote Scripture. They could all even quote Paul. Some advocate theories that stress the moral example Christ provides as the one who embodied the reconciling compassion of God that ultimately triumphs over the enslaving forces of evil. "In all things we are more than conquerors through him that loved us."[6]

Other theories stress the forensic declaration of God that we are forgiven because the sacrifice of the sinless Christ for sinful humanity satisfies the sacred commitment to justice. "Since all have sinned and fall short of the glory of God; they are now justified by his grace as a gift, through the redemption that is in Christ Jesus, whom God put forward as a sacrifice of atonement, by his blood, effective through faith."[7]

Still other theories emphasize that Christ was our representative as the Son of Man, and as the Son of God he was the divine representative. On the cross this mediator atoned for our sins by bringing God to the godforsaken, and by uniting us with God. "For our sake, he made him to be sin who knew no sin so that in him we might become the righteousness of God."[8]

All of these theories use metaphors and symbols derived from battlefields, altars, courts of law, and classical philosophy to describe the gracious activity of God that can never be contained by any theory. To assert any one of them too stringently at the expense of the others is to miss some of the biblical teachings about the atoning death of Jesus. One thing about which all of the theories agree is that the center of our faith is Jesus Christ, and not a theological construction about him. Another thing about which they agree is the desperate need humanity has for a Savior. But the most important claim found at the center of all orthodox theories of Christ's atonement is the benefit of forgiving grace, namely, that we are restored to communion with God. In the words of theologian Colin Gunton, "the center of the doctrine of atonement is that Christ is not only our substitute—'instead of'—but that by the substitution he frees us to be ourselves."[9]

The church may not be exactly clear how grace works, but that is only because it is God's gift and thus beyond our capacity to categorize. The point of forgiving grace is not to understand it but to receive it. When we begin to accept this grace from God, we turn away from the hell of alienation and start finally to walk in freedom.

Until nomads are transformed by grace into pilgrims who can begin this journey, they experience freedom only as slavery. In his classic book *Escape From Freedom*, psychoanalyst Eric Fromm demonstrated that in a free society a person simultaneously "becomes more independent, self-reliant, and critical, and he becomes more isolated, alone, and afraid."[10] His thesis in the book is that the anxiety and loneliness created by freedom eventually becomes overwhelming to the individual who then chooses to sacrifice freedom to new dependencies that offer security. This, he claims, accounts not only for the rise of modern totalitarian societies but also for the dehumanizing effects of democratic societies.

Fromm's hope was that the modern people would learn to refuse to make this sacrifice and heroically assert a true individuality that does not "conform to anonymous authorities" any more than it would to fascism. A generation after he made this proposal, we are living in a postmodern era in which more permission than ever before has been given to assert this true individuality. But to what ends? We nomadically wander into one conformity after another. The only thing that has really changed is that we can now easily exchange our taskmasters. We move from being defined by one job and relationship we hate to another. Some even make heroic efforts to get out from under the debt that has bound them to this alienating lifestyle in order to start over. They go back to graduate school, learn a new trade or profession, remarry, completely reorganize their lives, but soon the old anxieties surface, and it is not long before they find themselves back in the same mire of conformity they worked so hard to escape.

As Dostoyevsky's devilish Grand Inquisitor said to Jesus Christ, "There has never been anything more difficult for man and human society to bear than freedom. . . . In the end they will lay their freedom at our feet and say to us, 'Enslave us, but feed us!'"[11] But it is no longer our anxiety about food that keeps enticing us back into conformity and slavery. It is now our anxiety about finding a life. The more freedom a society offers the individual to assert the true self, the more taskmasters that individual will find to serve. Even the permissibility has become enslaving. Since the nomads *can* go to another place, they feel they *have to* go in the relentless search to find a life they want. But somehow they just keep ending up back in Egypt.

The freedom to express true individuality comes not from asserting the self, but from asserting the power of salvation to all who live in Christ. What is at the center of our hope is not our individuality, and not even our longing to have that individuality saved, but the relationship between the Father and the Son and the Spirit who proceeds from them. Everything necessary for our salvation out of the hell that addicts and conforms us to so much less than we were created to be is accomplished by the work of the Triune God. That's why it is called grace. All that remains for us to do is to express our gratitude by walking away from hell and heading for home, where we are finally free to be ourselves.

COMING TO OURSELVES

The first thing Virgil does after leading Dante out of hell is wash his tear-stained face, "restoring it to its true color." That is because there is no redemption to be found in looking like a man "buried underneath the dirt of hell," once he has been freed to turn and come home to paradise.

Virgil cleanses the pilgrim's face in response to the instructions of Cato, the first person they meet on the other side of hell. Cato was a first-century Roman Stoic who was well known for his stern moral principles. He is presented in *Purgatory* as a type of Moses, complete with a long white beard, who has come down the mountain to embody the law. Virgil introduces the pilgrim to Cato saying, "May it please you to welcome him—he goes in search of freedom and how dear that is, the man who gives up his life for it well knows."[12] It is only in losing the hellish life of separation and alienation for which we had settled that we find our freedom to move toward being new creations. And only the vision of this freedom can inspire us to lift our eyes beyond the misery we know.

Cato is impressed by this journey, because it was always the purpose of the law to condemn the alienation created by our sins, and neither the pilgrim nor the pilgrimage home. So it was Cato who told Virgil, "Go with this man, see that you gird his waist with a smooth reed; take care to bathe his face till every trace of filth has disappeared, for it would not be fitting that he go with a vision clouded by the mists of hell."[13] Even the law is a grace that calls us to journey, looking not at the mists of our hell but the hope of our paradise. When the pilgrim was making his way down into hell, his waist was girded by a rope, which he lost along the way. For Dante, the rope is an image of strength that ironically binds us to our sins. After leaving hell, that rope is replaced with a smooth reed, a classic symbol of humility. We didn't get our freedom because we earned it but because we were forgiven.

According to Revelation, another vision of the future meant to give insight to our pilgrimage through this life, Jesus is depicted saying, "Behold I have set before you an open door and which no one is able to shut. I know that you have but little power, and yet you have kept my word and not denied my name."[14] The freedom to continue to the place where we are truly ourselves is found not in our power but in the name of Jesus the liberator, who mercifully opens a door out of hell that no one can shut. Not even our own sins. But we have to choose to walk through it. The moment we do, we are not home because there is still a long way to go on the journey before we arrive. But neither are we lost. We can't be lost if we know where we're going.

The church of Jesus Christ is never made up of anything more than those who were once lost in some stifling hell but have walked through the open door named Jesus Christ and have now begun the freedom journey back to God. As Jesus kept trying to explain to the religious leaders of his day, nothing will get in the way of that journey quite like refusing to admit you were ever lost, because then there is nothing from which to turn, and without turning we can never make it through the door. Dante's inferno was filled with religious leaders who trusted not in the forgiving grace of God, but in their own discolored robes roped in self-righteousness. The striking thing about these leaders is that even in hell they were still too tied to their own hubris to walk out by a door called grace.

From the perspective of Scripture, the primary tragedy when this happens is not found in the lives of those who enslave themselves to hell, but in heaven that longs to rejoice when lost slaves are found walking in freedom.

Once, when Jesus was trying to explain to the Pharisees why he spent so much time with sinners, he began to tell some parables.[15] In the first one a shepherd leaves his ninety-nine sheep to find the one that is lost. He searches the wilderness, and upon finding the sheep he says, "Rejoice with me for I have found the lost." In the second story a poor woman loses one of her ten silver coins. She tears the house apart looking for it, and when she finds it she also says, "Rejoice with me for I have found the lost." After both stories Jesus makes the point that heaven is filled with joy when a single lost sinner turns around and repents. Then Jesus told his third, and most famous, parable about the prodigal son.

A man had two sons. The younger one (it's always the younger one) said to his father, "I want my share of the inheritance right now." There was no ancient custom of a father giving his children their inheritance before he died. What this boy is asking for is outrageous, and the implications of it are outrageous as well. Essentially he is saying to his father, "I can't wait for you to die." But what is most outrageous is that the father gave the kid what he wanted and divided his assets between his two sons. Interestingly, this means that the elder son benefited from his brother's impetuousness.

The elder son then maintained his share of the family property, which was probably the larger portion. He worked the land, lived conservatively, and preserved the family estate. But the younger one liquidated his assets, fled his father's house, and traveled to a distant country.

We don't know where that place was because when Jesus told this parable his only point was to say that it was a distant place. Every place we wander finds its relative value to us only in being distant; in other words, it is not the Father's house where we are known and cherished as his children. We fled because we didn't really believe that we were his beloved, and so we tried to find our lives and freedom some other way.

In the distant country the prodigal used his pseudo-freedom to squander his birthright in "dissolute living." That's the sanitized version. Later we learn from his elder brother that he blew it all on prostitutes, hoping to find an alternative way to be beloved. It was not long before he was spent, enslaved, and found himself having to feed hogs in the distant country—a tough way to hit bottom for a Jewish boy. He became so hungry that he considered eating alongside the hogs. This is anything but a picture of authentic freedom.

That's the problem with the distant country. Even if you are economical with your resources and do not live carelessly, you will still find that it isn't long before the distant country uses you up. As long as you are not home, you are on the run, and you can only run for so long. Eventually you run out of achievements, jobs, resumes, health, and new ideas for self-improvement. Then you just feel spent.

It was when the son came to this bottom of his life that the memory of the father's house returned to him, and then he "came to himself." Remembering that this is not who he is, not really an alien or a hog, he decided to turn and begin the journey home. The grace in this story is found not only in the moment that the father received him back and restored his identity but even in the memory that allowed the son to come to himself and turn around.

I have seen this parable replayed a thousand times. Someone comes to Washington, primarily because it is not the place where they are known. For a while they enjoy all of the excitement and power, but it is not long before these things drain their lives. They do things they never thought they were capable of doing and spend so much time slopping the hogs that they start to act like a hog. It's amazing the things you do in a distant country. But at the bottom, grace appears and the memory of the Father's house returns. This is not a memory of the house in which they were raised but the memory of paradise that has persevered on their souls. So they come to themselves, maybe wander into a church, and begin the journey home.

The prodigal knows that he has made huge mistakes in the distant country and he doesn't deserve to have a place in his father's home. But he is hungry, there is no place else for him to go, and the memory of his father's house will not leave him alone. So he starts down the road home. As he does he rehearses the lines he will use when he gets there. "Father, I have sinned against heaven and before you; I am no longer worthy to be called your son; treat me like one of your hired hands."

Like this prodigal, along the way home we tell ourselves we could never be what we once were. We would settle for so much less than paradise as long as it's not the hell we knew, but eventually we'll discover that grace follows grace and it is the Father's prerogative to choose to restore us. None of that happens until we first come to ourselves, remember the Father's house, and head home.

"But while he was still far off," we are told, "his father saw him." How many days had the father wandered down that road that led away from home and tarried awhile at the gate? How many times did he look up from the fields and gaze across the horizon, searching for his lost son? How long has the Father in heaven looked "far off" in hopes of our repentance?

Then one day he saw him—beaten, ragged, tired, shuffling his way home —and the father tore down the road, with his robe flying in the wind behind him. He threw his arms around his boy and showered him with kisses. The poor kid doesn't even get to finish his little speech before the father cries out, "Quickly, bring my best robe, a ring, and sandals for his feet. Kill the fatted calf. Let us eat and celebrate." Then again, for the third time, we hear the words. "Rejoice with me, for I have found the lost."

That is what happens every time we repent. We start out the journey for home rehearsing new deals we will make with God. But the Holy Spirit interrupts us to say, "Heaven is rejoicing because the lost is found." Remember this celebration was not the prodigal son's idea, but the father's. If we are paying attention we are embarrassed by the grace we receive when we come home. It doesn't matter. The Father is so excited he commands rejoicing.

The elder brother, who is usually so good at obeying commands, has a hard time with this one. He is placed in Jesus' story to embody the Pharisees and Scribes who refuse to enter heaven's celebration over the return of the sinners because it just isn't fair. They're quite right about that. It isn't fair. When the father comes to his pouting eldest son, he doesn't try to justify his younger brother. He does remind him of the relationships, calling the eldest his "son," and the prodigal, "your brother." Then the father reminds the responsible eldest son that he has always been home. "All that is mine is yours," he says. But the eldest, who never left, has really never been at home because he had been trying to earn what had already been given to him.

No country is as distant from the Father as the land of pride.

Finally, the father invited the eldest son to come home—to the place of rejoicing. Come to the place where love isn't earned, but is given away. Come to the place where those who are lost in the sins of immorality and greed are joined to those lost in the greater sins of hubris and self-righteousness. Come to the place where you are home, and where the grace is always extravagant.

We don't know if the elder brother repented of his pride and joined in the joy or not. Perhaps that is by design, so we can finish the story with our own choices. But before any of us write those final lines, remember that the point of this parable is not to be right, or careful, or to do a good job with life. The point is to come home to the Father's arms. And we can only get there by grace.

THE FATHER'S HOUSE

Trying to prepare his disciples for their own journey to the Father's house, Jesus said, "In my Father's house there are many dwelling places. If it were not so would I have told you that I go to prepare a place for you? And if I go to prepare a place for you, I will come again and take you to myself, that where I am there you may be also."[16] This is one of the most frequently used texts in funerals. I have written many homilies on it myself, to proclaim our hope that in death the Savior takes us to himself, where we are able to dwell in the Father's house forever. That is a good and faithful use of this text, but it is incomplete, for Jesus is saying more about the Father's house than pointing out the final destination to the journey of repentant sinners.

Jesus concludes his first paragraph by saying, "And you know the way to the place where I am going." Thomas, who always had trouble catching the metaphors, responded, "Lord, we don't where you are going, how can we know the way?" It is then that Jesus says, "I am the way, the truth, and the life. No one comes to the Father except through me." His point is that the way to get home to the right place, the place where we can finally abide and find our life, is through his communion with the Father.

Shortly after this, Jesus begins to explain how this communion is made possible through the ministry of the Holy Spirit who will abide with us, even after the Son returns to the Father. Under the power of the abiding Spirit we are so bound to Jesus Christ that we can continue to follow him and share in his communion with the Father, even though he now sits at the right hand of the Father. But our participation in Christ's way means not only that we will one day enjoy his full intimacy with God, it also means that we can appropriate that as we continue on the journey toward home.

This is the thrilling part! Jesus claimed, "Those who love me will keep my word, and my Father will love them, and we will come to them and make our home with them."[17] The Father isn't just waiting in paradise for us to get there, but has run down the road to find us along the way. He was present through the memory of his house that graciously returned to us when we came to ourselves, and he was present even when we were too blinded by the hell to which we fled to see him. This is why the Apostles' Creed affirms that Christ descended into hell before ascending into heaven. If nothing else, it means that no matter how low we descend in life there is no place that the grace of God does not abide with us.

The prophets had long foretold a time when God would choose to dwell among his people.[18] That future apocalyptic hope has now been realized and made possible through the indwelling of the Holy Spirit, who not only brings us home to God but who also brings God home to us. So we journey, not as lonely pilgrims in search of our home, but as sons and daughters of the Father who enjoy dwelling in sacred communion with God along our earthly sojourn. That is why we are never lost, because we are never away from home even as we journey toward it. We carry the Father's house in our mortal souls, like prodigals who have come to ourselves and realize we cannot escape its memory. So we head for the home that never left us.

The Father's house is another symbol, albeit a biblical one. Like all symbols, it cannot contain the full nature of what it tries to symbolize. What Jesus means by invoking it is not to limit God to a particular gender. There are other biblical texts that utilize feminine symbols for God, but those do not mean God is a woman any more than the texts that refer to the sacred wings mean that God is a bird. We do not project a mortal understanding of fatherhood onto God, but rather derive our understanding of both masculinity and femininity from the God in whose image we are made as male and female. It is also in this derivative sense that Jesus uses the term, identifying himself as the Son begotten of the Father. And it is in a derivative sense that we understand our home as being not the one we create for ourselves, but the one created by the call to dwell with Father, Son, and Spirit.

From my pastoral conversations with those who had a difficult childhood experience with absentee or abusive fathers, I know that it can initially be difficult to make sense of this biblical symbol of the Father's house. And for those who are committed to speak inclusively to a society that has for too long oppressed its women, it can seem inappropriate to still use this language about the Father. However, to avoid it makes both a theological and pastoral mistake.

The theological mistake is that avoidance dismantles the Trinity, which has been revealed to us as an eternal relationship of persons: Father, Son, and Spirit. To speak only of the Creator, Redeemer, and Sustainer, as is in vogue today, reduces the persons of the Trinity to their functions and thus severs the interrelationships between them. The home to which we belong and in which we find our true identity is not just another place of function but a communion of relationships. So we call God our Father because the Son did, and it is into their relationship that the Holy Spirit adopts us as sons and daughters. We have no language in this family apart from the one given us by the Son.

The pastoral mistake in refusing to use Trinitarian language is that it is precisely those who have had terrifying experiences with earthly fathers or oppressive experiences with patriarchy who are most in need of the symbol's redemption. The Father's house is not simply another house run by an angry or insecure man, but it is our true home where we are honored as cherished sons and daughters.

When my father abandoned his family to nomadically wander his life away, I was still a teenager. For a long time I struggled through the darkness of feeling disposable. The only biblical light that could break through that darkness was the realization that my real Father would never leave or abandon me. "Those who love me will keep my word, and my Father will love them, and we will come to them and make our home with them." That's the only home we can never, ever lose.

No matter how dark the house was that we are fleeing on our way home to the Father, and no matter how hellish the hurts we received at the hands of others, the last thing we want to do is to allow those hurts to blind us to the vision of the redemptive home. In the words of Cato, "take care to bathe his face till every trace of filth has disappeared, for it would not be fitting that he go with a vision clouded by the mists of hell."

"I hold these keys from St. Peter, who advised:
     'Admit too many, rather than too few,
      if they but cast themselves before your feet.'"

Then pushing back the portal's holy door,
     "Enter," he said to us, "but first be warned:
      to look back means to go back out again."

Dante, Purgatory, IX. 127–32, p. 100

7

Climbing the Mountain
The Road Home Is Hard

It takes a while to get home. Actually, we spend all of the rest of our earthly days just trying to make progress on the journey. We continue on the journey the same way we began. By grace.

TRAVELING LIGHTLY

I was in the airport, standing quietly beside other weary travelers in that little circle of prayer that always gathers around the baggage carousel at the end of a flight. Eventually a buzzer blared, the little red light on the carousel started blinking, and the bags began to tumble down the chute, one after another. As I watched the bags circle around and around, I was overcome with a sense of déjà vu. What did this feel like? Then it hit me—pastoral counseling.

Seldom do people make an appointment with their pastor to say everything is fine and they're just so grateful they can't stand it. No, they come to see the pastor when they are weary from their journey in life. For a while they may have checked their baggage as they flew through another new job or relationship, but they know the time has now come to take possession of their issues, and they're looking for spiritual help. As they talk, one by one, the bags start to appear. It usually isn't long before the parent baggage comes down the chute (that's a big one), followed by the self-esteem baggage, and the bag marked "unsatisfying work." They may want to talk about their dreams, which is the baggage that somehow got lost. There is always at least one bag that has the word "HURT" scrawled across it, as if to warn others to handle this one with care.

As we continue to talk, the same bags just keep circling around and around because they aren't particularly attractive and no one really wants to claim them. Every time I think that we are done with an issue, it soon becomes apparent that it was only out of sight for a while and has now returned into view. It took me a while to discover that many of my parishioners are thinking that I'm the skycap who is going to lug all that baggage away for them, which is not really my job. So I just listen. But when the time is right, I do invite them simply to walk away from it all.

The journey home is difficult, and no one who is burdened by excessive baggage makes it to the end. The hardest thing to leave behind isn't really our many possessions, but the guilt and hurt we have collected as souvenirs from the hard places we have wandered. Periodically, it's necessary to have something of a garage sale of the soul to get rid of that stuff.

When Jesus was preparing his disciples for the long road of ministry that lay ahead, he told them, "Be on guard so that your hearts are not weighed down."[1] Don't overload them, he warned, because whenever the heart is full it cannot handle another thing. Not even a Savior. Some of us have heavy hearts because we have taken on too much pathos from the tragic lives of others or the world that is crying out for hope. But most of us can fill up our hearts with our own pathos. We just can't believe the things we have done and all the hurt it has caused. Some days it feels like the heart is so heavy that it will pull us back into hell. So we have to unload all of that guilt or we'll never make it home.

It is interesting that Jesus never said, "Be on guard that your hearts are not too light." Perhaps that's because while some forms of shame and sadness prevent us from seeing Christ, all forms of joy help us see him. It is just too hard to laugh with your head down.

Progress on the journey home is measured by how far your face has turned from down to up and thus from the mists of hell to the light of glory

When I was a college student, I spent my summers working in a hiking camp, taking groups of boys up and down the Adirondack Mountains. Those who were new to this form of "adventure" tended to overstuff their backpacks with things they really didn't need. It wasn't long on the journey before their shoulders and backs were hurting like crazy. So they walked slowly and tilted forward, which kept their heads bent down to the ground. They were more focused on their muddy boots than on the top of the mountain that was getting closer and closer, and they missed all of the beauty along the way because they weren't looking for it. And they complained. All they could think about was how tired they were, and they wished they had never signed up for such a demanding climb.

This is why Jesus told his disciples, "Take nothing for your journey, no staff, nor bag, nor bread, nor money—not even an extra tunic."[2] At first we would wonder why Jesus would send us out so ill-prepared. But he was calling us to put our trust not in the things we carry, but in the Savior who will carry us.

That's how we make it home. We don't trudge along on our own dogged strength, but we are carried up the mountain as we discover more and more of our need for the grace of God. It doesn't matter how much baggage we carry, we will never be equipped for the journey home, and the more baggage we have the slower we will move. But it is precisely when we feel ill-equipped for the journey home that we are ready to make progress. Then we are in a better posture to pray, not as weary nomads bowed down by the burdens we have collected on all the detours we've taken, but as pilgrims who are free to look up for salvation.

As Virgil explains to those doing penance in purgatory for their pride, "O haughty Christians, wretched, sluggish souls, all you whose inner vision is diseased, putting your trust in things that pull you back, do you not understand that we are worms, each born to form the angelic butterfly, that flies defenseless to the Final Judge?"[3] Purgatory is the allegorical place that describes how we fulfill the purposes for which we were born—to be transformed from crawling worms into butterflies who travel home on wings.

MAKING SENSE OF PURGATORY

It is hard for many Protestants to understand the doctrine of purgatory, but I find that often Roman Catholics are as puzzled by it as Protestants. But Dante presents it as symbol that is accessible for everyone who is ready to leave the hell of alienation and begin ascending the mountain toward home.

The earliest record we have of teaching about purgatory comes from the third century. The early church fathers Clement of Alexandria and Origen both make reference to the need for a sanctification to occur in the lives of those who made deathbed conversions. That was largely because the church was still being persecuted in the third century, and those who had lived under this threat interpreted it as sanctifying blessing. Persecution focused the lives of the early Christians, helping them to remain devoted to what was so important that they would die for it, and purifying their lives from the distractions of culture that weren't worth dying over. For example, the martyrs were never tempted to define themselves as consumers. That's why it was a blessing. To avoid persecution and then convert to Christianity just before dying was to be robbed of this blessing. Thus, some believed, it had to occur in the next life. Augustine, writing over a century later, also spoke about the necessity of purifying pain in the journey between death and heaven. As the centuries continued, so did the development of the doctrine.

As with most things medieval, purgatory found its theological clarity in the writings of Thomas Aquinas. He claimed that while the guilt of our sin and alienation is already cleansed by the atonement of Christ, the wounds created by that sin remain and must be cleansed prior to our entrance into heaven. Purgatory is the place where that purification happens. Those who are in purgatory are distinguished from those in hell because they have turned from their sins and toward the forgiving grace of a Savior who removes their guilt. But the wounds left on their souls from their sin remain until they are healed by prayer, penance, and purgation.

Reformers Martin Luther and John Calvin rejected the notion of purgatory completely because they believed it lacked biblical warrant and because it seemed to be only a way of contributing to a salvation that was accomplished by Christ alone. It isn't our wounds from sin that remain after death, they claimed, but only the wounds of the risen Christ, which he showed to the disciples in the upper room.

If *The Divine Comedy* is perceived as a series of theology books, then Dante is just providing medieval instruction on purgatory that's only about the need for purification after death. But if it is seen as a collection of poems that are to be interpreted allegorically, then Dante is showing us how to continue in the journey of this earthly life without getting lost. We can all read the purgatory poems of *The Divine Comedy* the same way we read about the wilderness journey of the Hebrews on their way to the promised land. The Exodus is not literally our story, but we can certainly learn from the eternally rich images of leaving slavery behind, crossing a river, and heading for home. We don't immediately arrive, but spend a lot of time in a hard place along the way, where we are transformed from being runaway slaves into becoming a people who eventually walk by faith.

As depicted by Dante, purgatory is a mountain that has three stages. The first is antepurgatory, which is near the trail head. Gathered here are all of those who are not ready to begin their purification because they are the "Late Repentants." They wander aimlessly at the base of the mountain without any discipline or order because, having put off the grace of salvation that was offered in this life, they now have to put off paradise. It is as if to say, you can't begin the journey home until you begin. But that means stop wandering aimlessly and start your disciplined, focused climb home.

The second stage of the mountain accounts for most of it, and thus it is purgatory proper. It contains seven terraces that represent the seven deadly sins. In *The Inferno* these sins were organized as descending circles leading to the bottom of hell. Here they are presented in inverse order, not as addictions but as opportunities to gain more and more freedom. The pilgrim must participate in the penance that is occurring on each of the seven terraces of purgatory in order to learn how to turn away from his sins. With the prideful, who walk under weights that bow them down, the pilgrim is seen bending down to examine the floor. Later in the journey he enters the terrace of the wrathful, where he walks through thick dark smoke. And with the lustful the pilgrim has to makes his way through burning flames to get to Beatrice, with whom he has always been infatuated.

As the pilgrim continues to make his way up through the terraces, Virgil encourages him to stay focused and fly upward. But early on in the journey the gravity of his sin keeps pulling him down. The further he progresses, however, the easier it is to make progress on the climb. That is not because the pilgrim is earning his way, but because he is learning to have more faith in God's grace than he does in the gravity of his sins. When this weight is gradually removed, Virgil promises the pilgrim, "then will your feet be light with good desire; they will no longer feel the heavy road but will rejoice as they are urged to climb."[4]

At the top of the mountain is the third stage of purgatory, which is where the Garden of Eden is found. The pilgrim's climb has to finally return him to the earthly paradise before he is ready to enter into the eternal paradise of heaven. This is not to say that after death we will literally have to return to Eden, but only to claim that our prayer and penance is necessary because we have lost the primal innocence we were created to enjoy. No one can truly behold God in the eternal paradise when they are still suffering from this lost innocence. The fruit of our penance is that it prepares us for a fuller vision of God's revelation. It is this vision of God that guides our journey and finally brings us home, and we find it only by emptying ourselves of all the mists of hell.

DON'T LOOK BACK

At the entrance to purgatory proper, where the pilgrim and Virgil will start their climb through the seven terraces, they meet an angel who guards the gate. After carving seven P's on the pilgrim's forehead, representing the seven stages of penance, the angel tells him to use purgatory to cleanse himself of these wounds from his sin.

Wounds have a way of preoccupying us. They are among the worst of the baggage we carry on life's journey. When we are wounded we do not walk easily, but limp along in a way that defers and caters to the wound. We hold the wound, nurture it, and allow ourselves to even be defined as wounded people. But the reality is that we are what God created us to be, and that is not wounded. So the wounds have to be healed.

The worst wounds are self-inflicted.

Pastors don't have favorite parishioners, but if we did, Jeff would be one of mine. By the time I met him he had already made a mess of his life. His addictions to alcohol, cocaine, and sex had already cost him two marriages, alienated him from his family, and dismantled his success at work. After crashing into the bottom of his nomadic life, he had begun the long process of recovery aided by several twelve-step programs. But in spite of working his way through the steps utilized by Alcoholics, Narcotics, and Sexaholics Anonymous, he was still struggling with guilt over all the people he had hurt along the way in his descent into hell. That's when he started to come to church, and eventually he made an appointment to see his pastor.

The lament that just kept flowing from his lips was, "I can't believe what I have done." When a pastor hears those words it is tempting to rush in too quickly and say, "Oh, but that is in the past. Now you are making better choices, and you have to stop thinking about history." But it wasn't time for those words. Jeff was trying to show me the wounds on his own soul that he had created by wounding so many relationships. So instead of encouraging him to ignore his wounds, I had to help him make his lament to God.

The reason he is one of my favorite parishioners is that Jeff knows how deadly it is to cover over a wound. The people who are most impeded in their pilgrimage are those who pretend they have no guilty wounds because they can't even understand why they're not making any progress. As Jeff gradually took more and more responsibility for all that he had done, accepted more and more of the grace of God, and tried to make amends as it was possible, the wounds ever-so-slowly began to heal. His courage to take responsibility for these wounds was directly related to his faith in his new identity. Knowing that he was now more than an addict, he could tell the truth about all the hurt he caused when he was—not the least of which was the old hurt that lingered on his own soul. That's what penance looks like. It has nothing to do with wallowing in our sins and everything to do with confronting the old wounds in order to turn from them back to a new identity of one who has found the cleansing grace of God.

These days it seems like Jeff is walking more lightly, smiling more often, and now the words that keep flowing off his lips are, "I'm just so grateful." He isn't exactly innocent again, but neither is he wounded by guilt.

The real poster boy for this deliverance from guilt is Paul. When we first meet him we are told that he was "ravaging the church by entering house after house; dragging off both men and women, committing them to prison."[5] After his conversion experience on the road to Damascus, he joined the church he was persecuting and soon became its missionary leader. Later, in the book of Acts, as well as in his Epistles, the story of his conversion is repeatedly told. The striking thing about these testimonies is that Paul never gives the slightest inclination of having guilt for all of the terrible things he did to the members of the early church. That isn't just because he writes it all off as the sins he committed before knowing that Jesus was his Savior. It is because he had experienced the ministry of the Holy Spirit, which was allowing him to live a new, guiltless life in Christ. That is what it meant to call Jesus his Savior.

The salvation Jesus offers us isn't just about wiping clean the slate of our sins. That only amounts to giving us a second chance, and we all need a whole lot more than that. Salvation means that the old life is dead, and in its place we are given the life of Christ. This new life is a reality from the moment of our baptism, where we were buried with him in baptism and raised to a new life, but it takes the rest of our journey to fully live into this new reality. As Paul explains to the Philippians,

> Not that I have already obtained this or have already reached the goal; but I press on to make it my own, because Christ Jesus has made me his own. Beloved, I do not consider that I have made it my own; but this one thing I do: forgetting what lies behind and straining forward to what lies ahead, I press on toward the goal for the prize of the heavenly call of God in Christ Jesus.[6]

Since the Savior is the one who claimed us as his own, our identity is actually nothing less than his as the beloved of the Father. As we respond to the heavenly call and keep pressing toward that goal, by grace we begin to embody new identity. Along the way, the vision of the heavenly home becomes more clear and the image of Christ becomes more revealed within us. Then, it finally becomes possible to forget the things of the past. Even the guilt. That is just one more thing that was exchanged for the righteousness of Christ. We can try to keep pretending that we are still wounded and guilty, but that will only slow us down on the journey. Only those who really believe they are the beloved of the Father will have courage to stop pretending to still be an old creature that has already died, and to come home.

When the angel in purgatory opened the door for the pilgrim and Virgil, he cautioned them not to look back because it would mean to go back. This is another reflection of the clear biblical teachings about the danger of looking back. That's what turned Lot's wife into a pillar of salt. Many have assumed that she was looking back with fondness for Sodom and Gomorrah, but the text doesn't tell us that. Maybe she was just focusing on her disappointments and heartaches from the city. Even more pressing are the warnings from Jesus that no one who puts a hand to the plow and then looks back shall enter the kingdom. We simply won't make it home if our faces are turned toward the hell from which we are being delivered. Paradise offers an upward call, and we cannot make the climb if we are facing backwards.

In *The Great Divorce*, C. S. Lewis describes a similar, but more modern, journey to the one Dante depicts in *Purgatory*. Lewis's story begins with a bus from hell that deposits ghosts at the base of a mountain. Walking up the mountain is hard on the ghosts' feet, but the more progress they make, the more real they become as Solid People and thus the easier the journey becomes for their feet. Many of the ghosts don't make it because their attention is focused back on the hell they have created for themselves. Halfway through the journey this is explained. "There are only two kinds of people in the end: those who say to God, 'Thy will be done,' and those to whom God says in the end, '*Thy* will be done.' All who are in Hell, choose it. Without that self choice there could be no Hell. No soul that seriously and constantly desires joy will ever miss it. Those who seek find. To those who knock it is opened."[7] The way we seek is by turning our face away from the former things and toward the top of the mountain.

At one point in *The Great Divorce*, Lewis introduces us to a ghost who suffers from a terrible lizard that digs its claws into his shoulder and makes the most terrible judgments about him. The lizard

hates this journey and wants the ghost to take them "home"—back
to hell. An angel is waiting to kill it, but the ghost first has to agree
to let go of the lizard. The thought of living without this thing that
has wounded him for so long is actually frightening to the ghost
because he has learned to befriend his tormentor. He tries to put off
the decision but realizes that he is now at a point in the journey in
which eternity depends on his choice. Although he is not at all clear
about what will happen to him after the death of the lizard, he decides
he's better dead than alive with this creature. So the terrified ghost
finally agrees to the death of the lizard. In a flash the angel slays it,
allowing the ghost to become a man and transforming the lizard into
a great white stallion that carries the man the rest of the way up the
mountain to his home.

Lewis's most profound point is that it hurt the man to have the lizard killed because its claws were in so deeply. Penance hurts. Becoming
a Solid Person hurts. Even turning from the lie that we belong in hell
hurts. That's because we have taken the lies too deeply into our souls, and
extracting them is painful. But it is also the only way that we are freed to
turn our face toward our true home. Just because it hurts doesn't mean it
won't lead to our salvation. And just because the road up the mountain
leads home doesn't mean it is easy.

THE LOVE THAT BRINGS YOU HOME

What Dante most wants to show us from purgatory is how to restore
the love that became sick when we lost our way. If the inferno was the
place where we learned to confess our failures with love, purgatory is the
place where we learn how to turn to prayer that our health may return.
Only then are we free to enter paradise.

Along the way up the mountain of purgatory, Virgil explains to
the pilgrim that there are two kinds of love that God places in our
hearts before we are born. The first is an instinctive love for God
that makes us want to return to him. The second kind of love is born
of our free will, and it can mislead us if we do not choose to love
correctly. But when free-will love is disciplined, it remains attuned
to the heart's instinctive love for God and refuses to attach itself to
anything that will pull us away from our home with him.

Since love has such a powerful place in the human soul, all actions are essentially born out of it, for either good or evil. For example, sloth is the sin of insufficient love for God or anything else. Greed, gluttony, and lust are caused by an excessive love for "secondary goods" and not the primary good of serving God. The purpose of all the penance and turning that people are doing in purgatory is to learn how to love correctly, by which Dante means recovering the love for God at the center of all our other loves.

He begins the poems about purgatory proper by saying, "we had passed the threshold of the gate forever closed to souls whose loves are bad and make the crooked road seem like the straight . . ."[8] When love goes bad it not only prevents us from continuing the journey home, but it also makes it seem like the wrong road is really going somewhere. This is illustrated in the confusion of contemporary nomads who spend their lives thinking that the meandering crooked road to the next place has to be the right road, simply because it leads to the next place. Their love born out of free will has somehow gone bad, allowing them to confuse the next place with home. But it can't be home, because whether they realize it or not, even nomads are created with an instinctive love for their home with God.

Like all medieval thinkers, Dante's understanding of love is essentially Aristotelian. It was Aristotle's claim that love is built into creation as the force that makes everything seek its own place. Why does the river run downhill toward the sea? Because it is trying to get home. That is also why the stars stay up in the heavens, and it is why souls are on a journey through this life. They are all motivated, drawn by love, to get home. Sin is thus perceived by Dante as a distortion of the created order of love that leaves us lost along the way. And purgatory is where we learn to turn from perverted love to its true object—paradise.

This holy business of learning to love correctly so we can find our way home is very difficult. It's usually accompanied by some form of crisis, because it is in the midst of overwhelming loss that we realize just how crooked and wrong the road was that we were traveling. Some of our psychologists have described it as the process of moving from naive orientation to disorientation, then to reorientation.

There was a time when life seemed to make sense, and the world appeared to be in order. You felt secure and believed that the world itself was not in any great danger. But this was only an illusion created by your love for the familiar. When a crisis occurs this naive orientation falls apart: the doctors find a terminal disease in your child, your company goes bankrupt and takes your retirement plans down the drain with it, your husband tells you he has never really been in love with you. Suddenly the whole world becomes dark.

Now you are in the stage of disorientation. What is grieved in this stage is not only the particular loss but also the lost naiveté that was rooted in a vision of God who you thought had the job of making things nice for you. That's because you had used your gift of free will to love secondary goods and not your true home. But there is no going back to stage one, no return to that immature illusion of life you once loved. The only way out of the crisis is to discover a more authentic vision of God.

As a pastor, I have found that people are tempted to despair when they are in a place of disorientation. My job is to tell them that there is actually more hope for them in this stage than there ever was in the illusion they once loved. There can be no room in the human heart for authentic love, the one that will bring us home, until we first have the illusory loves pulled out of us. But again, that really hurts. Climbing a mountain isn't easy.

The psalmist wrote, "My soul is cast down within me, therefore I remember you from the land of Jordan . . ."[9] When the naive orientation is cast down, it then becomes possible to recover the instinctive, creative love for God. That's the redemptive benefit of the crisis, because with the memory of God comes hope. As the psalmist continues, "Why are you cast down, O my soul, and why are you disquieted within me? Hope in God, for I shall again praise him, my help and my God."[10] Frequently this memory of God that returns in disorientation comes from childhood. Maybe from Sunday school, a mother who used to read Bible stories, or even a conversion experience one night at a campfire. A new love for God is discovered by pulling out of the ashes an old love that was always there but never followed. Now that the love of God is needed, it is received, and in receiving it we are able to give it. As we find ourselves directing the heart away from the naive world that was lost, and away from the naive vision of God, we are now able to love not only God but also others for their true value, which is rooted not in what we needed them to be for us but in their value to God.

This is when you reach the stage of reorientation in spiritual development. In this third stage you return to a place you have never been before. You return to loving God, but differently. No longer is God perceived for his instrumental value. That vision was lost with the crisis. Now the love is simply for God with no added benefit to it.

The people who have passed through this dark night of reorientation are the most free people I know. That is because they are no longer afraid of losing anything. It is all gone. All that is left is the only thing from which they can never be separated—the love of God. And with that clarity of desire, it is not hard to find the way home.

FINDING SUSTENANCE FOR THE JOURNEY

When the Hebrews left slavery in Egypt and were making their way through the hard lessons of the wilderness, which is another symbol of purgatory, they were sustained by the daily gift of manna. This was a "fine flaky substance" that came as the blessing of bread from heaven.[11] For the next forty years it served as the staple for the Hebrew diet. It had to be collected every morning, and everybody had to gather their own basketful.

Other than that, we don't know a thing about the bread from heaven. Neither did the Hebrews, who gave it the name manna because the word means, "What is it?" Every morning the mothers would gather some "What is it?" and place it on the table. Their children would ask, as they always do, "What is it?" and the moms would say, "Well, yes."

It is striking that their daily nourishment through the purgatory of the wilderness was found in a question. This means that the manna was something of a sacrament that offered a ritualistic way of renewing the terms of their relationship with God. As they took the manna into their bodies, they were also taking a question into their souls. "What is it, God, that you are doing? What are you asking me to leave behind, to do, to become?" Nothing is more nourishing for the soul than asking that question, because it takes the focus off of our dreams and resources, both of which have run dry, and it turns our faces toward the dreams of God that only he can deliver.

Some will say, "I thought that if I just got promoted to management, I would finally have the job I have always wanted. Now that I have it, I hate it. And it's too late to start over. So *what is it,* God, that you are telling me about work?"

Others will say, "We saved our whole life for retirement and had such wonderful plans for how we were going to use it. But now he's sick, and all of our time and money is spent on doctors. *What is it,* God, that you are doing in our lives today?"

Still others will say, "I have always been grateful that I lived in America because I felt so safe here. But now I am discovering that all of the violence of the world can invade our cities just as easily as others. *What is it,* God, that you are doing with our nation?"

These are the important, irresistible questions that we bring with us into prayer and worship. Authentic change in our lives begins simply by asking these questions of God, because the very act of prayer rehearses our dependency on the Savior. We thought that the new job, dream, or illusions about security would save us, but now we see that it was all just another way of perverting our love, and it hasn't brought us to the right place. Now, in the bottom of our disorientation, we remember that we were created to love God, so we have to ask how he will use all of this to bring us to himself. It is not our job to answer the question. That's God's responsibility, and he will fulfill it by the slow transformation of our lives. In time, we will see what God is doing, but by then we will feel less like worms crawling our way out of slavery and more like butterflies who are carried home on the gentle breeze of new mercies.

Later in the wilderness sojourn, some of the Hebrews got fed up with the uncertainty that had become their daily regimen of grace. So they started to complain saying, "If only we had meat to eat! We remember the fish we used to eat in Egypt for nothing, the cucumbers, the melons, the leeks, the onions, and the garlic: but now our strength is dried up, and there is nothing at all but this manna to look at."[12] As any nomad can tell you, a prayer that begins with the words "if only" is very dangerous because you may receive what you want, and then how will you explain your unhappiness?

We are told that it was the rabble among the Hebrews that got them complaining. This was a group that they brought with them from Egypt who were not true believers in God or in the transformation he would bring to their lives. In Cecil B. DeMille's movie *The Ten Commandments,* the rabble were personified in the character played by Edward G. Robinson. Every time the going got difficult, he was the guy who kept saying, "Yeah, Moses, where is your God now?" Soon another riot would break out. The rabble's toleration for discomfort was low, and their capacity for complaint was high. That's both an unfortunate and infectious combination. It doesn't take much for the "strong craving" of the rabble to get everyone worked up into a lather of anxiety. That's when they all began to say, "If only we had meat to eat."

The most dangerous rabble are not the complaining people around us, but the rabble that lives in every human heart. It's as if we have a tiny little Edward G. Robinson in there who keeps tempting us to be anxious, making us doubt God's love for us, and thus our devotion to him. Since there are so many voices in our heart, all screaming for our attention, we have to choose which one we will obey. As Dante was trying to explain in purgatory, and as Moses explained in the wilderness, the really frightening thing is that God will honor the choices we make with our free will.

Responding to the craving for something other than sacred questions, God said, "Fine. You want meat? I'll give you meat until it comes out your nostrils."[13] Then he sent hoards of quail which the people devoured until they literally choked on it.

If asking "What is it?" is the means by which our faith in God's transforming work is nurtured, then complaining, "If only" may be seen as the anti-manna. When we ask questions of God for which we are not given immediate answers, we find room for faith to grow. Faith is what binds us to God when we don't see how all of this is leading us to the right place in life. Nothing is more deadly to that developing faith than turning our faces back to Egypt and saying, "If only."

Sometimes we say those words because we are focused on the future: "If only I could get a better job." "If only I could find someone special in my life." "If only I could afford to retire early, then I would be okay." Sometimes we use the phrase because we are focused on the past. "If only I had my health back." "If only I had my husband back." "If only I had back the money I put in the market last year, then I would really be okay." Speaking these words preoccupies us with either the future or the past. It assures us that our happiness lies in those places that implicitly define our present life by what is missing. Thus, the words "if only" are always a judgment upon the present day.

One of the greatest dangers in contemporary society is that we are losing the present tense because things are moving so quickly. Within a few generations we went from traveling around on horses to jet airplanes. The miles that used to take months to cross we now cover in minutes. Our computers move so fast that we have to speak about nanoseconds, because a second is no longer a short enough unit of measurement. Our children are hustled through life at the same breakneck speed. Within nanoseconds of getting to high school, someone starts talking about college. *If only* they could get into a good college. Then they're out the door. "What was it that just blitzed through our home? Oh, it was our children."

Psychologically this has the effect of reducing the present tense to being nothing more an anticipation of the rapidly approaching future. In my grandfather's generation the present lingered for a while as it stretched relatively unaltered from a distant past to a distant future. Today the past is much less prescriptive, the future is much less remote, and the present scarcely exists at all. But remember, the people who could not see the present tense were all in the inferno. And according to purgatory, our preoccupation with either the past or future is only more baggage that we have to lose along the way.

Here's the great danger: when the present tense disappears in your life, so does the manna. The mysterious, life-giving, blessed grace of God only comes in the day you have. If you miss that daydreaming about the future or longing for the past, your soul will never find its only source of nurture and you'll never survive the journey. Without the ability to see what God is doing today you are always anxious, never at home, and thus never joyful.

The ninety-fifth Psalm depicts God's response to those who complained their way through the journey by constantly lamenting "if only" and living in a day other than the one they were given. The Lord said, "For forty years I loathed that generation and said, 'They are a people whose hearts go astray, and they do not regard my ways.'"[14] Throughout the Bible we are given this same consistent message. Nothing grates on God quite as much as our complaining. He doesn't respond as strongly to our many other sins, even idolatry, as he does to our complaints. God just loathes complainers. That's because they will never find their way home by complaining that the road is hard. It's supposed to be hard. That's what turns us to God.

"I lead you here with skill and intellect;
    from here on let pleasure be your guide:
    the narrow ways, the steep, are far below. . . .

Expect no longer words or signs from me.
    Now is your will upright, wholesome and free
    and not to heed its pleasure would be wrong:

I crown and miter you lord of yourself!"

Dante, *Purgatory,* XXVII. 130–32, 139–42, p. 294

8

Forks in the Road

It's Not about Our choices, but God's

I t is typical for nomads to be very worried about their choices. This anxiety is created not only by the vast number of choices they have to make but also by the nagging suspicion they will not choose well and will end up in the wrong place. Again.

Every road leads to a fork, and every fork in the road eventually leads to another. But all of the roads belong to God. The real challenge is not choosing the correct fork, but learning to walk with the Savior who can use any road to bring us home.

CHOICE OVERLOAD

Kate is a twenty-nine-year-old attorney who works for a large firm in Washington. She was raised by conservative parents who worked hard to put her through college and a prestigious law school in Boston. When they were living in the Midwest, her family was very involved in a Bible church, which she remembers fondly as a place that "really believes in the Word of God." Halfway through Kate's high school years, her father moved the family to the West Coast to take a better job. They never got involved in the new megachurch they attended, but everyone in the family really enjoyed the exciting worship services.

When she went to college she experimented with a latent-adolescent rebellion, stopped attending church, went to a few beer parties on campus, and got "a little too intimate" with a guy she was dating. But none of that lasted long. By her sophomore year she was involved with an evangelical student group on campus and a year later was asked to join its leadership.

She went to law school in Boston, where she also participated in the singles' ministry of a local church. She became involved with a young man she met there. After graduating she moved to Washington to begin her career, which meant moving away from her boyfriend. Since then the two of them remained as close as the distance would allow, but they were both feeling the time had come to make a commitment or break things off.

She had been a member of our congregation for about two years, after trying another church in town for the same amount of time. In addition to singing in our chancel choir on Sunday mornings, she attends a large Sunday evening contemporary praise service at a different church, and she had recently been on a mission trip to Peru with a parachurch organization that she financially supported. She's a typical Christian nomad, trying to find the right place.

When she plopped down into the chair in my study, she sighed as if to tell me she had been carrying the weight of the world on her slim shoulders. There was no small talk. She began, "I just want to know what to do." "About what?" I asked. "Well, pretty much everything," she said, sighing again. "Oh," I said, "this may take more than one appointment." But she was not amused. This was not the first time Kate had come to see me, and I had a hunch this was going to be as intense as our previous conversations.

"There are just so many decisions, and I really don't know the will of God for any of them. I'm working seventy-hour weeks at the firm because that's just what it takes to make partner. But sometimes I wonder if helping my clients make more money is exactly what God has in mind for my life. I could get a more reasonable job with the federal government, but frankly, the money stinks and the work looks pretty dull. My boyfriend has a great job with his parents' business back in Boston, and he doesn't want to leave it to move here. I guess I could move up there, but to tell you the truth we are both uncertain if this thing is going to lead to marriage, and it seems kind of silly for either us to move just to work on a relationship. I love that guy, but I just don't know. When I look at the older women who are partners in the firm, they aren't exactly the models I want for my life. But I'm really good at this work and think that someday I could be one of our litigators. And I haven't even got to the whole issue about children, which is the only thing my parents seem to think about."

I just let all of that confusion hang in the air for a while. Then I said flatly, "You have a lot of choices."

She fired back, "You think? I really like all your sermons on grace, pastor, but I wonder if you are giving people enough practical guidance. I mean, I'm facing really critical choices in my life, and after being a part of your congregation for two years I still don't know what to do. I'm more accustomed to churches that provide very specific direction from the Bible. I'm very good at following the rules, but I have to know what they are."

I waited again, hoping to slow her down.

"How would you react," I finally asked, "if I told you that it was the will of God for you to give up your job, move to Boston, and hang out with your boyfriend?" Kate responded, "I would wonder about all the invest-ment my parents and I made in bringing me this far in my profession. And I would ask you why God made me good at this kind of work."

"Okay," I said, "and how would you respond if I told you that it was God's will for you to dump the boyfriend and commit yourself to this job?" Another sigh. "I know what you're trying to do," she said. "Of course, then I would have to tell you that life is more than work and if I'm going to take this relationship seriously I have to take it seriously. So your point is that I would question your advice no matter what you told me."

"This isn't a cross examination, counselor. My only point is that when you reduce God's will to things like job descriptions and your dating life, you may be missing the bigger picture."

"The grace thing again, right?"

"Absolutely. God's will is that you glorify him and enjoy him forever. I'm wondering how much you are enjoying God with these choices. Or are you only fearing that you may disappoint him?"

"Of course I fear that," she exclaimed. "When I broke the rules my first year of college, I hurt God and I hurt myself. And I don't ever want to go through that again."

"I'm not saying that there isn't clear biblical teaching for how we conduct our lives, but I don't think you're going to find a verse in the Bible that tells you if you should work for a firm or the government, stay here or move to Boston. Maybe the Bible is telling you more about the need to be grateful that you have choices, to make them humbly and prayerfully, and to believe that God is still the Creator of your life no matter what decision you make."

"It can't be that easy," Kate lamented.

"It's not easy at all. It is hard work to take responsibility for your own life and to see all your choices as opportunities for loving God. On the cross, this God stretched out his arms to you and said, 'I'm dying to give you life.' It seems to me that the best way to express your gratitude is to accept the gift of new life, and pray that the Spirit forms you more and more into the life of Christ. Ultimately God is much more concerned about your character than your job. Maybe you are fretting over the wrong choices. Maybe the real dilemma is what does it mean to live in Christ?"

"I know all that stuff," she said. "What I don't know is what God wants me to do." And that was the last time I saw Kate.

THE DIVINE SHRUG

We are living in an era in which we are confronted by more choices than our grandparents could ever have dreamed of having. We can choose our professions, relationships, the number of children we will have, if we'll have them, where we will live, how we will live, and with whom we'll live. Not only can we make these choices but we have to make them, which is what reduces our freedom to just more stress.

Kate is typical of those who are intimidated by their own freedom, and who just want to know what to do. I've had this exact same conversation repeatedly with other devout nomads. Having lost a sense of home, they don't know what to do and are hoping now their church home(s) will tell them.

Kate was accustomed to a Christianity that peddled certainty for decision making. The interesting thing is that nothing from this "faith" background was working for her as she confronted her choices, which is ironic since she treasured it for its specific guidance. She had been taught to believe that God wanted her either in Boston or Washington, but it was not clear which place. This terrified her, because it meant that behind her choices about work and relationships was the dilemma of deciding which fork in the road would carry her to God. When I tried to get her out of this mindset in order to think more about God's will for her character, it just made no sense. I guess it really doesn't if the faith has been reduced to map-reading skills.

The reason we want our faith to help us read the map for life's journey is because we just keep encountering forks in the road. It doesn't matter how old we are, periodically we find our way to another fork in the road. That is because each fork leads only to more forks. The choices we are making today are the direct result of the choices we made yesterday. The middle-aged banker is confronting different choices than the middle-aged teacher or the middle-aged parent who decided not to keep working outside the home. And it's all because they each made different choices twenty years ago.

We are not unaware of this, and so we think long and hard every time we come to a fork in the road. We really want to end life in the right place, but we don't actually know where that place is or what road to take to get there. So we are often confused at the forks. In fact, we're more than confused. We are terrified of making a mistake. We think that if we make one wrong choice on one of these forks we are doomed to land up in a place called Nowhere Special. Or if the landscape on the road on which we're traveling has become dreary we worry, "I made the wrong choice back there and now look where I'm heading. I have to get off this road. Soon!" These are the fears that lead people to make an appointment with their pastor.

When I listen to nomads tell me about all of their choices, I'm actually struck by their blessing of having so many opportunities. They could go to law school or medical school, stay home with the kids or keep working, take the new job or keep the old one, move to the retirement home or keep the big house. "Well, isn't it wonderful," I want to say, "that you're not a medieval serf worried about the Black Plague?" But I don't say that because I have learned that a nomad is too frightened to be grateful.

Since they are coming to talk to their pastor, the assumption they often have is that I will help them discern what choice God wants them to make. When we finally get to that point in the conversation, I usually shrug my shoulders, smile, and as profoundly as possible say, "I dunno." It is at this point that they realize why pastoral counseling is free. But just to drive home the point I will often add, "Do you really think God is up nights worrying about whether you are going to be a policeman or a fireman? Maybe even he is shrugging his celestial shoulders on this. Maybe he just wants you. If he has that, then he can't lose on the vocational choices."

GOD OWNS ALL THE ROADS

We are not the first persons to ask questions about direction. Thousands of years ago King David wanted to know the same thing when he wrote the twenty-fifth Psalm. He begins this psalm, this prayer, as we do. "Make me to know your ways, O Lord, teach me your paths."[1] He might as well have said, "Show me the right fork in the road to take."

Just to be clear, David was not struggling over vocational choices when he wrote this. That was pretty much settled for a king. What he was concerned about was finding the right paths to God. "Lead me in your truth," he continues, "And teach me, for you are the God of my salvation; for you I wait all day long." When we scratch off the veneer of our confusion about jobs and relationships we find that our souls are wrestling with a far more existential confusion: "Why isn't my life working out as I had hoped?" "What do I do with all the guilt or the hurt I keep lugging around?" "Where do I really belong?" Now we are asking questions that God does worry about a great deal—questions that, in Jesus Christ, he was dying to answer.

Although this is lost in the translation, the twenty-fifth Psalm was written as an acrostic with each verse beginning with the next Hebrew letter in alphabetical order. Even in this prayer, David was looking for some sense of order in his disordered life. And that is exactly what he finds as he continues to pray: "Be mindful of your mercy, O Lord, and of your steadfast love, for they have been from of old. Do not remember the sins of my youth or my transgressions; according to your steadfast love remember me for your goodness' sake, O Lord."

In the words of the old pietists, prayer is a means of taking shelter under the broad folds of a sacred mantle that covers all who bow their heads before God. Surrounded by this loving mantle, you are left with "a peace that passeth understanding." My grandfather used to speak frequently about this peace that passeth understanding. But we don't hear that phrase so much anymore, and that's a shame, because it is exactly what we are searching for when life is confusing. What we need is a peace that goes beyond understanding since understanding is exactly what we do not have and may not get for a long time. We can live with that confusion, but only if our souls stop churning.

As G. K. Chesterton has written, "We can understand everything only by the help of what we do not understand."[2] When we no longer attempt to contain God to a particular fork in the road, and see him less as a traffic cop and more as the wild and sacred Lover of our souls, we are free to see that the fork in the road is just a fork in the road.

In the words of Yogi Berra, when we come to a fork, it's best to take it. That's only possible if we understand we can't choose our way outside of the sacred love.

This is how confused nomads find the cherished peace that passeth understanding. It's the same way David did—by allowing the Holy Spirit to move our prayers beyond our desires to encounter the desire of God, we remember his steadfast love. Psalm 25 begins with a request for direction but moves quickly to a soulful renewal under the mantle of God's love. Similarly, we may begin our prayers asking, "What about my job?" or "Where is this relationships going?" but if we are listening in prayer we'll hear the still, small voice of the Spirit telling us "I love you."

If we know that, if we are again convinced that we are loved and forgiven by God, we also know we'll be okay no matter what happens. That is because we now understand that our lives will end up in the right place not because of our good choices, but because of the choice God made to love us. And this love is waiting for us on either fork of the road. Having been renewed, through prayer, in the merciful love of God, David then says, "All the paths of the Lord are steadfast love and faithfulness." This means God owns all the roads. Option A and option B both belong to God, so we can't miss him along the way regardless of which option we choose.

If God wants you to be a butcher, baker, or candlestick maker, you're not going to be able to miss it. C. S. Lewis claimed that God uses all the wrong roads to get us to the right places. If you believe that God owns all the forking roads, and that if out of his gracious love God has already chosen to lead you home to a future filled with hope, then you are free to make the best choices you can without anxiety that your soul is on the line every time you choose.

When I was a teenager in youth group our well meaning leaders used to torment us with the warning to be sure our choices were always the "perfect will" of God for our lives. "Be sure you pick the right college and job, and marry the right person," they told us. "Be sure you have discerned God's perfect will, because if you miss it you will be stuck with God's second best for your life." And oh, how we worried about getting second best, which means we were always panicked to know the will of God about everything.

Such anxiety is hard on the soul. It leaves a pilgrim paralyzed, making it impossible to head for home, and that is clearly not God's perfect will.

Second-best theology is a heresy. What we now teach our kids in our own church's youth group is that, in Jesus Christ, God has already given us the very best that he had to give. When you receive that gift and believe that in Christ you too are the beloved of God, then you can boldly make choices. If they don't work out well, then make different choices, because you now believe that God has already made his choice to bring you home on any of these paths.

After defeating death, the risen Savior can appear on any road we are walking, and he often will appear in the places we least expect him—like the road to Emmaus, or the road to Damascus, or the road to work. Every time he appears it is to remind you that you are not alone on that road. Seeing that, you are transformed from a confused nomad into a visionary pilgrim because it is the presence of Christ that gives meaning, purpose, and even delight to the journey. In the words of Oswald Chambers, "It is this intense reality of expecting Christ at every turn that gives life the attitude of childlike wonder that he wants us to have."[3]

Why do children enjoy their choices more than adults? Because their world is still filled with wonder. Ugly ducklings can turn into swans. A frog can become a prince. You don't know, you'll have to kiss it to find out. If their wonder ever turns to confusion, fear, or hurt, they have only to climb up into a lap to be loved until the hurt is gone. That is what prayer offers—time in the lap with Abba Father where confusion and hurt is loved away and the wonder of life restored.

The pilgrim's calling is not to get to the right place. That's the calling of the Holy Spirit in our lives. Pilgrims are called to look for and witness the wondrous things that Jesus is doing on the road we are traveling today.

LET PLEASURE BE YOUR GUIDE

When Virgil, the reasonable guide, finished bringing the pilgrim safely through all seven of the terraces of purgatory, he indicated his usefulness was almost over. Soon it will be Beatrice's gracious compassion that brings him into paradise. That is because reason can only take us so far on the journey home, and in the end it's the revelation of divine love that carries us inside.[4] Virgil's job, as commissioned by Beatrice, was to guide the pilgrim down into the depths of the inferno where he would confront his sin, and then up through the terraces of purgatory's mountain where he would learn to turn away from the things that made him turn from God.

Having arrived on the shores of Eden at the top of purgatory, Virgil announces to the pilgrim that now his own pleasure shall be his guide. "Now is your will upright, wholesome and free, and not to heed its pleasure would be wrong." These are startling words to us. We would expect that someone who has just survived all of the penance of purgatory would have had all of the pleasure prayed out of him. But Virgil would say that is an irrational expectation. The point of the journey home is to learn how to turn our passions into prayer, that they may be trusted and that we may follow the desires of our heart without peril.

When the Southern novelist Ellen Glasgow described her Presbyterian father who had an exaggerated sense of duty she said, "He was entirely unselfish, and in his long life he never committed a pleasure."[5] That's the stereotypical depiction of the religiously minded. But the purpose of authentic religion is just the opposite—it is to show us how to transform pleasure until it is no longer a temptation, but a guide that can bring us home.

Like any parent, the Father in heaven delights in the delight of his beloved children. It was never his intent to drive that capacity out of us. To the contrary, that is what we have learned to do to ourselves when we wandered away from home and accommodated our capacity for pleasure to lesser things than we were created to enjoy. Now that the pilgrim has prayerfully returned to Eden, he is ready to enjoy all of the pleasure of paradise known to Adam and Eve. That is when we were most fully alive, and to walk through this earthly life with even a vision of paradise means that the last thing we want to do is cut pleasure out of our hearts. It is impossible to be at home with God without knowing pleasure.

In the words of King Solomon, "Eat your bread with enjoyment, and drink your wine with a merry heart, for God has long ago approved of what you do."[6] This doesn't mean that God approves of all human choices. It means that long ago, when we were created, God called our passion to live with pleasure a good thing. From where does the longing for pleasure come? From the God who created us in his image, and who "takes pleasure in his people."[7]

It is amazing how much of the religious agenda is based on the assumption that God is really angry. Religious leaders devote themselves to debates over how we can appease this anger and what we must do, or stop doing, to prevent God from being mad at us forever. But this depicts God as a fragile, emotionally vulnerable victim who is not in control of his own feelings. And it reduces our spirituality to a codependent obsession with doing whatever it takes to make the angry God happy again.

God's anger over our sins is appeased by his own pleasure in us and not by our acts of contrition. That doesn't mean that we shouldn't be contrite for our sins, but it does mean that our sorrow is created by the discovery that in sin we have turned from the God who, in Christ, was dying to love us. The relationship between God and us has always been secured not by our frantic efforts to get back into his good graces, but by the goodness of his grace that precedes anything we would do, good or bad. Only when we received this grace are we free from fretting about the merits or demerits of our lives and able to turn our attention to the higher pleasures.

The nomads are lost not because their appetites for pleasure are too great, but because they are not great enough. They are lost because they settled for the next thing instead of the higher thing and for the illusions of the next place instead of the promises of home. We were created to behold beauty, delight in truth, love intimately, and to well up with tears every time we hear music so tender it could have only been learned in heaven. But we have blinded our eyes, closed down our hearts, and stopped up our ears because we're afraid such intense pleasure could never be found. So instead we pull out the credit card and buy a new boat.

Jesus walked away from all of the normal ways in which people find these unpleasurable pleasures. He left his house, the carpenter's workshop, money, comfort, and even the opportunities the people presented him to become their earthly king. But that allowed his heart to be filled with heaven's pleasures: blessing a child, extending the joy of a wedding reception, seeing the sick healed, the hungry fed, and the sinner forgiven. That wasn't just his job as the Messiah. It was his pleasure in watching heaven break into the hearts of mortals.

It never occurred to Kate to ask herself what she really wants to do. She is torn between her sense of obligations to work, parents, boyfriend, and even all of the churches and ministries through which she roams. She has become the poster girl for the over-achieving, under-living nomadic Christian who has made the tragic mistake of believing that faith is only one more demand that she construct her life just right, which is actually the best way to get it all wrong. Life isn't something we achieve, but a gift to be received from the Creator who gradually unfolds our lives along the way.

As Virgil explained to the pilgrim, rationality and careful decision making can only take us so far. There must also be a holy sense of imagination, delight, and love that accompanies our reason, and in the end takes us further than the limits of reason. This is what Chesterton meant when he claimed, "Poets do not go mad; but chess-players do. . . . The madman is not the man who has lost his reason. The madman is the man who has lost everything except his reason."[8] Without the guide of a holy dream, and the capacity to recognize the pleasures that give us a glimpse of heaven, we will simply go crazy when we hit the forks in the road.

It's not about the road. It is about the Spirit who proceeds from the Father and Son to find us on any road and transform us into the Son's own beloved relationship with the Father. Sanctifying our pleasure is just one of his favorite ways of providing this miracle. As the transformation occurs, we are carried closer and closer to home.

CROSSING THE RIVER

As purgatory proclaims, there is a need for a cleansing from the wounds we created on our souls when we lost our vision of heaven and went crazy. For some the madness was manifested in spiritual paralysis, while others went nuts searching around in life looking for the right road. In either case the result was alienation from God, and even alienation from our own souls that are only at home with this God. That's the deepest wound. We may have hurt others and hurt ourselves by our many sins, but nothing hurts as deeply as the alienated soul.

There is a time for confessing what we have done to ourselves, which is what hell forces upon us, and there is a time for turning from this sin, which is what purgatory and the wilderness experiences of life invite of us. But then there comes a time simply to forget about it.

When Virgil turns his pilgrim over to Beatrice on the shores of Eden, she first accuses the pilgrim of wasting his talents and straying from the truth. At the root of all his sins, she claims, was that he had abandoned his love for her, the embodiment of sacred grace.[9] The pilgrim responds, "My fear and deep chagrin, between forced out of my mouth a miserable 'yes'—only by ears with eyes could it have been heard . . . the recognition of my guilt so stunned my heart that I fainted."[10] But this last rebuke is not meant to judge the pilgrim. Rather, it was to proclaim that from which he has now been delivered.

The pilgrim, who can not even remain conscious when pondering his guilt over the past, is then taken to the River Lethe, which means "oblivion."[11] Having been baptized in this river, even to the point of drinking in its water, the pilgrim emerges out of it without any memory of his past sins. On the other side of this river he now sees Beatrice smiling at him. At the end of all the confession and repentance, it is not judgment but a gracious smile that is waiting. The pilgrim's greatest pleasure is to behold such grace. "My eyes walled in by barriers of high indifference, were drawn to her holy smile—they were entranced by her familiar spell."[12] Now he cares about nothing but the grace. It has always been there, as the familiar spell, but he could not see it until the wounding memory of his sins was washed away into oblivion.

Following this, the pilgrim is then taken to a second river called Euone, a Greek word meaning "well minded." After passing through these waters the memory of all his good deeds in life was restored. The order in which the pilgrim experiences these two baptisms is important. As he was told at Lethe, "If one does not first drink here, he will not come to know the powers there."[13] There is no way to recover from the madness and find a well-minded memory of life's goodness until the memory of our guilt is gone and we have beheld the grace of God.

The allegory of these symbolic rivers depicts a truth that is drawn from the core of the Christian understanding of baptism.[14] We will never be good because we have made good choices or lived the good life, but only because by grace we have been given the identity of the sinless Christ. When we continue in sin we are only pretending to be someone other than ourselves; who we really are is who we are in Christ. Having passed through the waters of baptism, even if it happened as a child, the old person is washed away to oblivion, and the good is recovered because it is the good of Jesus Christ. To walk through this life as a person who is not lost is to cherish this real and true identity of being the good and beloved child in whom the Father takes such pleasure.

So instead of worrying about finding the right road, we ought to be focused on the right river—the one that creates new life. You don't travel a river like you do a road. You travel in it, because the river is not passive like a road. It does all the work of carrying you to a new place, the right place, the place in the Triune Family.

If I had been given the opportunity to explore this point further with Kate, I would have encouraged her to trust her baptism. Having passed through those waters, she was essentially declaring to the world that her life was not her own achievement, but was the achievement of the Holy Spirit who was not nearly done recreating her. As her new life began with water, so will it continue. Those baptismal waters will bring her all the way home, some days through churning rapids and on other days as a gentle stream but always toward her heavenly home. The best that she can do is hold tight and take pleasure in the ride.

> From those holiest waters I returned
> to her reborn, a tree renewed, in bloom
> with newborn foliage, immaculate,
>
> eager to rise, now ready for the stars.[15]

The glory of the One Who moves all things
    penetrates the universe, reflecting
    in one part more and in another less.

I have been in His brightest shining heaven
    and seen such things that no man, once returned
    from there, has wit or skill to tell about;

for when our intellect draws near its goal
    and fathoms to the depth if its desire
    the memory is powerless to follow;

but still as much of Heaven's holy realm
    as I could store and treasure in my mind
    shall now become the subject of my song.[1]

             Dante, *Paradise,* I. 1–12, p.1

9

Is God Homeless?

The Transformation from Nomad to Pilgrim

I t is useless for nomads to try to stop moving and stay in one place. They're nomads. Even if they could stop moving, it would only endanger their souls.

When Dante's pilgrim begins his ascent into heaven, the very first thing he tells us is that it is God who moves all things. That's because redemption comes not from settling for a particular place, but by allowing meaningless, nomadic wandering to be transformed into a purposeful pilgrimage toward the holy realm.

THE NOMAD'S BLESSING

The contemporary nomad has grown up in a society that has so thoroughly inculcated the values of change that it is impossible to get rid of the lure of the road. None of us are going to return to the naiveté and mythology of the 1950s suburb, and we certainly

135

aren't returning to the severity of the farms and tenement dwellings of the inner city. We can't. Those days are gone, and there is no way to climb back into history to join those who settled into a particular place without gazing down the road, wondering where it may lead.

Millions of us still live in rural communities, but not as our ancestors did. We do not suffer like our grandparents through long, hard days, relatively isolated from the rest of the world. Even the most remote rural village in the Third World now has access to television and the Internet. With the spread and affordablity of these technological advances, the changing world has invaded every corner of the globe, making it impossible for anyone to avoid being caught up in these changes. They just keep coming. The efforts of fundamentalists around the world to gain the political power necessary to stem the tide of these changes are illustrative of how far and effective the changes have become. And the failure of these movements to succeed in permanently pulling their societies back to an era where life was easier to control is illustrative of the inevitability of change and the autonomy of the forces that bring it about.

This is seen most clearly when one looks not at the global society but at the typical home where the parents wonder what in the world is happening to their children. Well, the world is exactly what is happening in them. When their teenage son milks the cows, wearing a Walkman that plays the latest tunes he downloaded from the Internet, his head is being flooded with messages that will keep him thinking about more than the farm. Even if he never leaves the farm, he has already left the worldview of those before him.

While taking a mission tour through impoverished Palestinian villages, I never entered a home, no matter how humble, that was missing a television set. Repeatedly I saw young people wearing clothes bearing designer logos, including one woman who had a pair of Nike running shoes sticking out from under her burka. No matter how successful religiously motivated efforts may appear to be in covering this up, change will always stick out.

Similarly, millions live in the suburbs, but these are not the same suburbs to which our exile parents fled in search of a better life. Not only is this because of these same technological advances that broadcast the world through the three television sets and two computers that sit in the average suburban home, and the necessity of having at least two cars to wander back and forth through the family's varied commitments, but it is also because no one in the suburbs has the slightest illusion any longer that their community resembles the nation under God. The 'burbs are now perceived as bedroom communities where it is possible to find a better house for crashing at the end of a long, hard day of coping with the volatile world that keeps life moving at a very fast pace.

Since this better house costs so much, it usually takes more than one income to pay for it and all of the "necessities" that accompany life in these communities. That means that domesticity now has to be outsourced to maids, house cleaners, the lawn guy, and the pool boy, not to mention child care. Children don't come home after school to play, but are rushed off to soccer practice, piano lessons, karate, and SAT preparation classes. If Mom or Dad is around to ferry them to all of these places, they are fortunate, but often that's a luxury many parents simply cannot afford, so instead they ferry around their guilt between business appointments.

Some have attempted to step away from their long commutes and recover a sense of home with the creation of home offices. There is enormous momentum behind this movement today, as Americans spend three billion dollars a year on home office products and furnishings.[2] But some are beginning to wonder if instead of recovering a home this effort is not actually crowding out home with the demands of work that are now omnipresent in the house. The phone call from the business deal in Japan has to interrupt dinner because that's when the markets are open there. And when a small child toddles into the home office to ask for attention, it is just so tempting to say, "Not now honey, Daddy has to work." Several generations ago when shopkeepers lived above their stores, they turned the lights off at six o'clock, pulled the shades on the windows, locked the doors, and went upstairs where they remained until the next morning. But the home office has blended work and sanctuary into the same place, and it is always hard for sanctuary to survive in such a mix. If the work is demanding, which most work is, it is only a matter of time before the stress that used to be contained in the office is invited home. Add to this the stress that children lug around from their overly scheduled days, and everyone has plenty to share. Before long it gets all over every member of the family.

Clearly, we are not living in our parents' suburbs. Which is not to say their life was idyllic, but its illusion was. The reason our parents went to the 'burbs was to seek an alternative to the harsh, stressful life that was part of the fabric of the old farms and ethnic neighborhoods. Their hope was to build a better life for their families in communities that would truly be a part of the nation under God. But what began a generation ago as a search for a more convenient and ordered way of life has now spiraled into a footrace to keep up with lifestyles that are certainly comfortable but far from convenient or well ordered. Ask anyone who feels like they are losing the race and they will say, "No, I don't really think I'm living under God." But neither were their parents. Not really. They tried, but as the legacy of the suburbs reveal, it doesn't matter how carefully we plan, no one pulls the kingdom of God down from heaven by settling into a particular place on earth.

If our real home is with the Triune Family of Father, Son, and Spirit, then the way we find that place is continuing the journey toward God. The last thing we ought to be doing is settling for any place along the way. Blessedly, society is now changing so quickly that it is no longer possible to maintain even the illusion of stability. It may be that the conditions of life today are more conducive to the Christian life than in centuries past. The contemporary nomads, for all of the inner angst they feel about their lives, at least have the blessing of being discontented with where they are, and they are under no illusions that it is where they really belong. So they just keep looking.

Their yearning for another place can be redeemed as the longing for the true home. But this is not a home they will find; it's a home that finds the homeless.

THE WORD BECAME FLESH

Our salvation was embodied in the Son of God who left his home with the Father in heaven to be conceived by the Holy Spirit and born among people whose lives were far from settled. It is signifi-

cant that when this incarnation of God was born, he arrived in a
stable, not a home. Those who were blessed to witness this miracle—Mary, Joseph, the shepherds, and wise men—were also not at
home. According to the infancy narratives, those who remained at
home—Herod, Caesar, Quirinius, and the innkeeper—all missed
the miracle.

The arrival of Emmanuel, the God who is with us, was so quiet
and subtle that most of the world missed it. Even when we read
Matthew and Luke's accounts of it, the story is striking in its sim-
plicity. A very ordinary-looking couple, doing the very ordinary
thing of paying their taxes, are far from home and give birth to their
son along the way. That was nothing special. Ancient women gave
birth wherever they could—the back bedroom, the fields, a stable
behind a crowded inn. And yet with this birth, everything between
heaven and the chaotic lost earth was changed forever.

The Revelation of St. John shows us what this birth looked like
from the perspective of heaven, which was anything but subtle. It's
high drama. John's vision tells us nothing about shepherds or wise
men, and instead it depicts a dragon leading a ferocious struggle in
heaven. A woman clothed with the sun, wearing a crown of twelve
stars, cries out in pain as she gives birth. Suddenly the enormous
red dragon descends as his tail sweeps away a third of the stars. He
crouches hungrily before the woman, eager to devour her child after
his birth. At the last instant, the child is snatched away to safety as
the woman flees into the desert. The dragon is furious and takes
his anger out on the other children who remain behind.

In his Gospel, John also avoids telling us about the familiar
characters of the nativity and instead begins the story of Jesus' life
with the drama of creation. "In the beginning was the Word, and
the Word was with God, and the Word was God. . . . And the Word
became flesh and dwelt among us, and we have seen his glory, the
glory of a father's only son, full of grace and truth."[3]

Words are powerful. Words put together carefully can do a world
of good and words put together in anger can do a world of hurt.
When God first used the words, "Let there be," it was to push aside
the darkness and chaos and create room for light and beauty. But
just as the world continues to turn daily away from the light back

to the darkness, so do we. In a hundred different ways every day our hearts turn back to the dark chaos.

The Gospel according to John portrays a God who could no longer stand to see us living with so much darkness. Especially the darkness of our own making. God knows, the only thing that could restore us to life was a word as powerful as the words he spoke at creation. We needed a word that could help us be unafraid of the dark, a word about love and forgiveness that could bring us home. But a word like that cannot just be spoken. We've already heard too many other words by now that were hollow. People who promised to love us but they weren't there when we needed them most. We've heard words about a promising job, a promising lab report, a promising move to a new city. But in each case it turned out to be just words. Soon the darkness was back. If we were going to believe God's word, this time it had to become flesh and live among us. And so, as John tells us, God revealed the Word in himself—named Jesus Christ.

Most of the people of Bethlehem missed all this drama. They didn't see it from John's holy perspectives of either heaven or creation. All they saw was a humble country woman giving birth to her child. Some may have remembered that she fled to Egypt when she heard of Herod's anger. All would have remembered that Herod became furious and killed all the other children of Bethlehem. Tragically, not even that was out of the ordinary for them. None of them would have thought this was the work of the dragon trying to devour the Word from creation that been made flesh to dwell among them.

From the perspective of contemporary nomads, every night is just another night of exhaustion from serving Caesar, Quirinius, and Herod. It's just another ordinary year under the tyrants of boring jobs, broken hearts, and the inability to find a place where they can finally get a little peace on earth. But from the perspective of heaven there was high drama going on that silent night long ago that had the capacity to change all our nights and days.

It's the quiet intersection of the holy with the ordinary that is precisely our source for hope. If Jesus were born today it would be to another lost couple who were just as lost in the sea of nomadic disappointments and confusions. By his Spirit, that is exactly what does happens today. The Son of God is born again and again into the hearts of the homeless, which means divinity has made its home with those who are just quietly wandering through the dark.

G. K. Chesterton has captured this power of the subtle arrival of God in his poem, "The House of Christmas":

There fared a mother driven forth
Out of an inn to roam;
In the place where she was homeless
All men are at home.
The crazy stable close at hand,
With shaking timber and shifting sand.
Grew a stronger thing to abide and stand
Than the square stones of Rome.

For men are homesick in their homes,
And strangers under the sun,
And they lay their heads in a foreign land
Whenever the day is done.
Here we have battle and blazing eyes,
And chance and honour and high surprise.
But our homes are under miraculous skies
Where the yule tale was begun.

A Child in a foul stable,
Where the beasts feed and foam;
Only where he was homeless
Are you and I at home;
We have hands that fashion and heads that know.
But our hearts we lost—how long ago!
In a place no chart nor ship can show
Under the sky's dome. . . .

To an open house in the evening
Home shall men come,
To an older place than Eden
And a taller town than Rome.
To the end of the way of the wandering star.
To the things that cannot be and that are.
To the place where God was homeless
And all men are at home.[4]

SALVATION "EN ROUTE"

As the story of Jesus began, so did it continue. When he was thirty years old he left his home in order to walk our streets and enter into our lives, but unlike the birds of the air or the foxes who have holes, he never had a place to lay his head.[5] To all of those who dared to follow him, he warned that this would be the condition of their lives as well. His disciples had to drop their fishing nets, some of them even had to leave their father in the boat, in order to follow. He wouldn't allow one man to bury his dead father before having to respond to the call.

The four Gospels of the New Testament describe the most wonderful things that happen to people when they encounter Jesus en route. Repeatedly these stories of healing and forgiveness are introduced with transitional phrases: "As they were walking . . ." "Along the way . . ." "Then they came to . . ." "After this Jesus went to . . ." Even by their editing of the Gospel stories, the writers want us to know that redemption occurs on the road.

When Jesus was about to ascend into heaven he told his followers they would receive the power of the Holy Spirit to be his "witnesses in Jerusalem, all Judea, Samaria, and to the ends of the earth."[6] Thus the Spirit transformed the disciples into apostles, which means those who are sent out. But after the Spirit came upon them at Pentecost, the new apostles initially tried to keep the church at home in Jerusalem. So the Spirit then began to work through persecution resulting in the church moving from Jerusalem, all Judea, Samaria, and the ends of the known world.

A church that is filled with the Holy Spirit is never allowed to settle down. That is because the church is the body of Christ on earth, and Christ is on the move leading this world home to his Father. This is one of the fundamental distinctions between the Old and New Testaments. The Hebrews were a people of a particular place, who had a hard time worshiping God when they were not in that place. Their worship centered around a holy city that had in its midst a holy temple. And in the middle of that was the Holy of Holies, which was the meeting place between God and the people. So when Jesus began to describe himself as the temple of God that would be destroyed and resurrected, the Jews had no idea what he was talking about. What he was claiming was that he was the new meeting place with God.

After Pentecost, it eventually became clear that anyone who wanted to keep up with this new meeting place had to keep on the move. But their movements would not be aimless, because he promised that "Wherever two or three are gathered in my name, I am there among them."[7] So we travel through life as a people who know we are not abandoned. It was because he became homeless that we have the opportunity to find our home with him as a community that gathers along the way in his name and finds in him the way to their eternal life. It was for this reason that the community was called The Way before it came to be known as Christian.

Not everyone in the Gospels physically left home to follow Jesus, and not all first-century Christians became itinerant preachers and apostles. Nor were they expected to. As J. Ramsey Michaels has described the early church, "they maintained a continuity of interpretation if not of practice."[8] Even those who remained in their commitments to particular places were also sent out from the illusions of that place to nurture a new identity created in the new meeting place with God, called Jesus Christ.

When Jesus was crucified, the heavy veil that separated the Holy of Holies from the rest of the world was ripped from top to bottom, allowing the holiness of God to run out into all of the profane world. Seventy years later when the temple was destroyed, as Jesus prophesied, it was as if God was saying that he would never be contained to a particular piece of real estate again. Partly as a result of these historical events, partly by virtue of being a missionary community, and mostly because of the teachings of Jesus and the apostles, the early church spiritualized and transformed the commitments to the land they had received from Judaism. Thus, its vision has never been preoccupied with Jerusalem, but with the celestial city of the Heavenly Jerusalem toward which it is heading.

So when the church looks back to its Old Testament history, it would do better to draw as its model the tabernacle and not the temple. The tabernacle was the mobile meeting place with God that traveled on the backs of the priests as they wandered through the dessert. Even when they did not know where they were going, the important thing was to continue meeting God along the way. As they did that, they were slowly transformed from being merely wanderers into pilgrims who were ready to step into the promised land. The way this transformation occurred was through the discovery of faith in God along the way.

Faith nurtures our belief not just in a future promised land but in the God who leads us there and eventually to paradise. The promised land is not paradise. It's just another place along the way where we are called to serve as a kingdom of priests. God may lead us to particular places, jobs, and relationships where we are allowed to fulfill that calling. We may spend our lives there or have to move on to other places, none of which are ever going to be paradise. As the Old Testament reveals, there is plenty of hard work and discontent even after we enter a promised land. But even the discontent serves as a wonderful blessing that reminds us we were created for more than this. We were created for communion with Father, Son, and Spirit. No place on earth will suffice for a place in that Triune home.

So while we inevitably journey through contemporary society, we have the opportunity to be so much more than a people who settle for a place, and even so much more than meandering nomads who seek only the next place. We can be pilgrims who nurture the memory of the Father's house where we truly belong. We will never settle down, and certainly not expect God to settle down, but will travel through life as a part of the tabernacle community of pilgrims who are settled only in the certainty that the Savior is in our midst.

Those who have this vision of life discover the blessing of their life's meaning and purpose, which is simply to take the next step toward home. Their relationships, work, and care for others are always perceived as another step in the pilgrimage. That these relationships and workplaces are continually changing is neither inherently good or bad, but inevitable. Pilgrims are neither intimidated nor addicted to these changes, but see them only as the unexpected grace that prevents their souls from settling into anything other than communion with the one who is the same yesterday, today, and forever. The Alpha and Omega.

Pilgrims who have been on the journey long enough to be clear about their homeward vision will even perceive inevitable change as the opportunity to be changed themselves by God, who can use all things to bring them home to the place where their created identity is restored and they are finally themselves again. Paradise. Along the way, when two or three pilgrims gather in the name of their Savior, he is among them—which means they are never far from home. But the purer the vision pilgrims have of their Savior, the clearer they are that they do not yet resemble the body of Christ on earth. So they must keep moving, being changed, converted, transformed, by the vision of home they carry in their souls.

In the New Testament this movement is never affirmed simply for the sanctifying benefits of the individual pilgrim, or even the community of pilgrims who travel together toward their vision of the celestial city. The Gospels and Epistles have also called the people of The Way to demonstrate a sanctifying blessing to the places they serve, but not settle, along the journey. In his formative work *The Gospel and the Land*, W. D. Davies first demonstrates how the Christian gospel demanded a transcendentalizing of the territorial affections of Judaism. But he then concludes by reminding the reader that this gospel not only spiritualized holy places but also personalized holiness in Jesus Christ.[9] This means that the community that gathers around the risen Christ is never permitted to abandon its responsibility to any of the cities of the earth. To the contrary, since the source of holiness is found not in territory but in the Savior who is present whenever two or three gather in his name, the community that gathers around Christ must seek to participate in his revelation of holiness to all territories to which it is sent in mission, even to the ends of the earth.

THE HOUSEHOLD OF GOD

So the answer to the question, "Is God homeless?" is absolutely, and absolutely not. The incarnation reveals simultaneously that God is at home in the holy heaven above the dark, chaotic earth, and among the homeless of earth.

By becoming flesh and dwelling among us, God has found the lost and restored our communion by making his home with the home- less. But every experience of this communion is only approximate and makes us yearn for the full communion with Father, Son, and Spirit that we will know only when Christ takes us to the dwelling place he has prepared for us. In the meantime we will not settle for any other place, but will continue to follow this Word as a people of The Way. Home is no longer the place we are from, and never really was, but is now the place we are heading.

Through the Spirit, the Son is still present whenever we gather in his name as the holy presence that sanctifies not only his followers but also the places where they serve him along the way. This means that, in Christ, we have already found our home away from home.

As the visible, but often flawed, body of Christ on earth, the church exists as this home away from home. It's not the home we were looking for, but it is the place where the approximate com- munion with home takes place—just enough to make us really miss it. Even in the yearning, however, the memory of our true identity and mission returns. That's something only home can provide us.

When Paul was explaining this concept to the church at Ephe- sus, he called it the household of God. One of the most important things to remember about being a part of this household is that it isn't constituted by the members, but by Christ who has gathered into it those who were nothing more than alienated strangers. "Remember," Paul tells us, "that you were at that time without Christ, being aliens from the commonwealth of Israel, and strangers to the covenants of promise, having no hope and without God in the world. But now in Christ Jesus you who were once far off have been brought near by the blood of Christ. So then you are no longer strangers and aliens, but you are citizens with the saints and also members of the household of God"[10] Here Paul is demonstrating the transformation from the old covenant, which was all about a particular people being with God in a particular geographical place. The Gentiles to whom Paul was writing were strangers and aliens to that community. We too were strangers and aliens not only by the accident of our birth but also because we had simply wandered away from every notion of paradise that was written in creation and on our hearts.[11] But in the new covenant, we who were far off have been brought near and made members of God's household.

Our entrance into this household is based solely on the gracious activity of the Savior who brought us to his home with the Father, allowing us to leave behind the identity of nomads as we take our place in the pilgrim community that travels with God to God. And if the activity of Christ is what brought the church together, so is it what sustains the church and makes it more than a gathering of nomads who are all arguing about strategic visions to get the church to the next place. The church is not our home away from home because it preaches interesting sermons, has exciting worship, builds beautiful structures, or because its many programs cater to our felt needs. It is only the body of Christ to the degree that it finds its life, mission, and hope in Christ. There is no other basis for this household to exist, no other means by which it will serve the world around it as a sanctifying and redemptive presence, and no other hope for it to be the tabernacle leading us home. None of that is possible apart from being a community "in" Christ.

One of the reasons that Paul speaks so much about finding our life in Christ to the Ephesians can be found in the church's origins. When Paul went to Ephesus to nurture along the church, one of the things he must have noticed was the great temple to Artemis, one of the seven wonders of the world. But as a Jew, Paul wasn't even allowed in this grand structure. We know that there were also some temples for the pagan mystery cults, where worshipers participated in the dramatic life of heroic figures in hopes of receiving their strength. But Paul wasn't allowed in those temples either, which didn't bother him much because he never wanted the church confused with a mystery cult.

As he typically did in a new city, Paul began preaching in the synagogue of Ephesus. That went all right for a few months, but then he and the church got kicked out of the synagogue. So they had to start meeting in a lecture hall. For two years the church continued in this lecture hall with both Jews and Greeks hearing the Word of the Lord.

So the church wasn't meeting in the great temple of Artemis or the temples of the mystery cults, because the Jews among them weren't welcome. And the church wasn't meeting in the synagogue, because the Greeks weren't welcome there. They are not *in* the temple. They are not *in* the synagogue. Thus, it's not that surprising that Paul begins his letter to the Ephesians by reminding them that they are *in* Jesus Christ.

When the church makes settling into a place its priority—whether that is a geographic place, structural place, or place in its history—it is because it suffers from temple envy. But from the beginning that has never been where we belong. We belong in Christ, and he has always been on the move. So must his church as he takes it into all the earth where he is about his Father's holy business of finding the strangers and aliens and bringing them home. This means that the household of God is in a constant state of flux and change. What separates the pilgrim church from any gathering of nomads is not that our community is more settled and stable, but only that we have a holy purpose to our journey. That purpose is to be the home away from home, which not only offers approximations of Triune communion but also labors for approximations of the kingdom of heaven on earth.

The church cannot be Christ's sanctifying presence to the ends of the earth if it takes too seriously its own place or the place it is serving. To take too seriously its own place and holy fellowship is to resort again to the construction of a temple, and temples have walls that are meant to contain the holiness that God has already resolved to spread all over the earth. By contrast, when the church strives only to have the most dynamic music in its worship, the coolest social experience for its youth, or the loveliest building on Main Street, it is taking alienated culture far too seriously. What we must take seriously is God's love for the lost world, and only as the church manifests that love does it become Christ's sanctifying presence.

The household of God manifests its love not only by following Christ out into the world to heal the sick of body and soul, and not only by its many strategies for peace and justice, but also by bringing the stranger and alien into its fellowship. When the church is successful in this mission, it will mean that at times the boundaries between the church and the world around it will be hard to find. This means there will be sinners in the church. That is threatening to those who take the church itself too seriously and worry about protecting its holiness. But the whole point of the incarnation was that not even God worries about protecting holiness, preferring instead to dwell among those in need of salvation. Sin doesn't contaminate holiness, but holiness provides a means of redemption for sinners. Since the church finds its life in Christ, he is at its center, and a church defined by its center doesn't have to worry about the boundaries.

It All Holds Together

Not only does the incarnation mean that it is possible for us to live in Christ as members of the household of God, it also means that Christ has taken our alienation into himself. As Dante explains, "The human race lay sick below within their error for long centuries, until the Word of God chose to descend: there moved by His unselfish Love alone, He took unto Himself, in His Own Being, that nature which had wandered from its maker."[12] Or as Paul explains, in Christ all things hold together.[13]

When our nature "wandered from its maker," it wandered in a hundred different directions. The movement that is such a natural part of our lives today pulls us into many lives that seem disconnected and often even in competition with the other parts. Colleagues at work don't want to hear too much about our personal problems because it just isn't professional. When we return home, we try to avoid bringing too much of the office with us. But the contemporary nomad today isn't trying simply to balance work life with home life. The parts of our lives are legion, and all the parts move at the speed of light. Let us return to the suburban family discussed earlier in this chapter. Here's what a typical day looks like for the mother:

She wakes up in the morning with a start because she overslept from working too late the night before. So she jumps out of bed, gets the kids up, sits them at the breakfast table, and puts the cereal and milk in front of them. Somebody spills the milk and it goes all over her clothes. She gets ready to clean that off, but is interrupted as she sees her dog running across the street after the neighbor. She drags the dog back into the house, breaks up a fight between the kids, and searches for a lost shoe. After getting the kids off to school, she gives her spouse a peck on the cheek just before he jumps in the taxi that is taking him to the airport. Again. As she flies off to work, she only gets as far as the bottom of the driveway before remembering she has to take the dumb dog to the veterinarian, so she races back into the house, drags him into the minivan, and speeds off. After dropping the dog off, she gets caught in traffic and is really late by the time she hauls into the office. Her morning is jam-packed with computers that crash, copy machines that jam, and a legion of those little pink slips that say please call (but they don't really mean please). Trying to return just one of those calls sucks her into a black hole of a conversation she cannot escape, so she's late for a meeting down the hall. She rushes into the conference room and takes a seat only to have the person next to her say, "You smell like sour milk." Finally she gets out of that meeting that took forever and accomplished nothing, darts over to the fitness club, and jumps on the treadmill where she runs and runs and gets nowhere, as if that's not the metaphor of her life. Then she races out of the gym, and flies back home in order to pick the kids up. One of them has to be taken to soccer practice and the other to piano lessons. While they're there she dashes over to the grocery store to get something for supper, and then hauls back to pick up the kids from their practice and lessons. She hurries into the kitchen and makes something fast for dinner. Everyone sits down at the table, and just when she's about ready to take her first bite, one of the kids asks "Where is the dog?" So she tears back to the vet, gets the dog, and returns to a cold dinner. She then throws herself into doing the dishes, helping with homework, tossing laundry in the washer, paying bills, trying to fix the leaky toilet, and calling her mother, who says, "You aren't taking very good care of yourself," which is not exactly a news flash. Finally she falls exhausted into bed wondering how in the world she will ever keep it all together.

What would change if this woman was living in Christ?

She wouldn't necessarily be doing less, and may even be adding some household of God activities to her already crowded life. What would change is the compulsiveness that makes her look for her life in all of these activities. Is her identity found in being a wife, mother, daughter, consumer, professional, staying in good shape, running a taxi, or being a homemaker? It isn't found in any of them. Her identity is in Christ, which doesn't mean that she can drop her many commitments. It means that Christ has taken all of her wandering nature into himself, and thus he can be found in all of the places her marathon takes her in the course of a day.

There isn't one part of the world, or our fragmented lives, that is void of the presence of Christ. He is waiting at each stop in the journey, sanctifying every part of our lives with his holy presence. The pilgrim moves just as rapidly through life as the nomad. And the community of pilgrims known as the church changes just as frequently as the culture through which it travels. The difference is that the pilgrims aren't under any illusions of holding it all together. That is best left to a Savior. Our joy is found in the glimpses of him we get along the way. But when we see that, we start also to see all of the other blessings from home that Christ has brought.

As partners in a dance whirl in their reel,
 caught in a sudden surge of joy, will often
 quicken their steps and raise their voices high,

so at her eager and devout request
 the holy circles showed new happiness
 through their miraculous music and their dance.

Those who regret that we die here on earth
 to live above, have never known the refreshing
 downpour of God's eternal grace up here.

That One and Two and Three which never ends
 and ever reigns in Three and Two and One,
 uncircumscribed and circumscribing all.

Dante, *Paradise*, XIV. 19–30, p. 169

The Blessings of Home

Why Heaven Makes a World of Difference

A s Beatrice guides the pilgrim through paradise toward God, Dante makes some insightful claims about heaven, which are actually biblical claims about living on earth. The whole purpose of receiving a vision of the next life is to see this life from an eternal perspective.

Paul claimed that in Christ we have already received every spiritual blessing in the heavenly places.[1] Dante's *Paradise* is only a depiction of this same belief. Below are some of those blessings from heaven that remind us of home, guide our pilgrimage back there, and provide vision for life's journey along the way.

THE BLESSING OF A HOLY EMBRACE

Whereas the settler generation thought of heaven as being ahead of them, and the exile generation thought of heaven as being above them,

Dante claims that heaven is actually all around us. When he wrote *The Divine Comedy,* he was operating under Ptolemaic assumptions of the universe, which placed the earth at the center of all the circling planets and stars. As is typical of him, Dante inversed the significance of these assumptions and stressed not the earth at the center but the embracing presence of God beyond the furthest circle of the universe.

The cosmology of *The Divine Comedy* placed hell beneath the earth and the mountain of purgatory between earth and the ascending circling spheres of paradise. He claim that around the earth rotates the Moon, then Mercury, Venus, Sun, Mars, Jupiter, Saturn, and the stars. Each concentric circle of these planets includes all within it, and is governed by its own hierarchy of angels. Beyond the eighth sphere of the stars exists the Primum Mobile, which is the ninth sphere and the outer boundary of the universe. This realm is described as pure motion. It both contains and communicates all of the motion to the lower spheres. Encircling this Primum Mobile is the home of God, which Dante calls the Empyrean. By contrast to all that it contains, the Empyrean is immeasurable in size, spaceless, and motionless. It's a place of perfect peace and pure spirit. It is here that souls find their final, eternal home with God.

When this cosmology is placed next to Dante's Christology, it becomes clear that he is not just offering metaphysical speculation, but important claims about the realities of daily life. If pure holiness exists at the outer reaches of the circling universe by virtue of creation, and if holiness exists at the core of human life by virtue of the incarnation, then everything on earth is also holy by virtue of both the cosmic and christological embrace. This even includes those things, and people, that have lost their ability to reflect this holiness. Nothing exists outside of heaven, and all things hold together in Christ. Thus, nothing is beyond God's holy reach. Not the demanding supervisor, client, or parent. Not the terrorist. Not the hurt from the last place we stopped on life's journey, and not the disappointments that inevitably wait at the next place we rest. North and south, east and west, mountain and valley, past and future, good and evil, us and them—it's all held within the embrace of God.

This means that all of our pilgrimage through this life occurs over holy ground. When Moses stumbled onto the burning bush, he was told to take off his sandals because he was standing on holy ground. But before he saw that bush inflamed with the presence of God it was already on holy ground. It didn't look like it. It looked like the ordinary bush that he had probably passed a thousand times while he was taking care of sheep. The flames didn't make the ground around the bush holy; they only revealed its holiness.

Only after Moses saw that the place where he was already standing was holy was he able to accept the calling to go to another place with the assurance that God would be with him. He would even go to Egypt, which was the last place he wanted to go, because he learned at the burning bush that God owned Egypt just as he did the desert. Thus, pilgrims travel from one place to another not in order to find holiness, but because they have already seen that it is all holy and they cannot roam into a place that is void of God. Their calling is never less than to give witness to the sanctifying presence of God in the new place they have been sent.

If you want to quit your job and move to another town to take a different job, go ahead. God will be waiting in the other place for you. But just don't abandon the place where you are because you think it isn't holy enough. God is also where you are now, which means you have all the reason you need to hope because anything can happen in a place where holiness resides.

The church today has learned to divide the world between the sacred and secular, assuming that the secular components are not inherently spiritual. While this distinction may be useful to sociologists who measure the impact of religious values on a society, it is a distinction that is totally foreign to the Bible. The only biblical distinction we are given is between the sacred and the profane. All things are created as gifts from God and thus have a sacred purpose. But by virtue of the gift of human freedom, we can profane that sacred purpose by manipulating the blessing for something other than glorifying the Creator. Profane language takes words that were meant for blessing others and twists them into a curse. Making love can either be an almost sacramental expression creating one flesh, or it can be profaned into nothing more than "doing it." And when we view our work as anything less than a sacred mission, we profane this created capacity into being just a way to make money. It was all created for holy purposes, remains contained by the holiness of heaven that encircles it all, and has been sanctified by the Word made flesh that dwells in its midst. It may not look that

way, but that is true only for those who do not see from the perspective of heaven.

THE BLESSING OF TRINITARIAN DERIVATION

Since everything in heaven and on earth is encircled by God, it all
derives its existence from him. The primary derivation of this existence
for creation is sacred love, and the source of the derivation is the love
shared by the Father, Son, and Holy Spirit.

Given his affection for the circle, Dante utilizes it instead of the
triangle when he is symbolizing the Trinity. The Spirit is reflected in
the lower three circles of paradise, the Son in the second three, and
the Father in the upper three circles. But each is intricately related and
entwined into the other through the circles of love they share. "That
One and Two and Three which never ends and ever reigns in Three and
Two and One, uncircumscribed and circumscribing all."[2]

Describing the love he witnesses being shared between the Father and
Son, the pilgrim in paradise uses language reminiscent of the prologue
to John's Gospel. "Looking upon his Son with all of that love which each
of them breathes forth eternally, that uncreated, ineffable first One has
fashioned all that moves in mind and space in such sublime propor-
tions that no one can see it and not feel His Presence there."[3] The love
shared within this Triune Family is the creative force that has fashioned
all things, which means that the Son wasn't just God's Plan B for our
salvation, but was with God and was God from the beginning. Out of
the love between the Son and Father, the Spirit proceeded and hovered
over the darkness and chaos creating light and beauty in its place. This
means that love is woven into the fabric of creation, and certainly into
the fabric of the human soul created in the image of a Triune, inherently
loving God.

To pay close attention to authentic love is to attend to the God from
which it came. As John explained in his first epistle, "God is love, and
those who abide in love abide in God, and God abides in them. Love
has been perfected among us in this: that we may have boldness on the
day of judgment, because as he is, so are we in this world."[4] We live in
this world, not void of love nor waiting to be loved in the next life, but
we live as the Triune God lives—in love. We may not act loving or even

recognize the love that has created and sustained us. But the lack of love in our own lives is only what all of the confession and repenting is about on our journey home. The purpose of the holiness to which we aspire is to have love "perfected" in us. Authentic sanctification leads to authentic love. As Jesus kept explaining to the Pharisees, any form of holiness that is not loving is not derived from God. Conversely, any form of love that does not draw us closer to the holy God is not authentic love, because he is the source of love.

Just as the love flows down from God into the human heart, so does that love seek its home back in the heart of the Triune God from which it came. And as we continue on the journey, getting closer and closer to the home of the Sacred Family from which we came, that love transforms and perfects our lives. This isn't something we can do to ourselves. As Dante's pilgrim states when he is finally able to behold fully the Triune circle of love, "I yearned to know how could our image fit into that circle, how could it conform; but my own wings could not take me so high."[5] No one ascends into the loving communion of God apart from the Spirit who brings us there. Like all of the blessings of heaven, love cannot be achieved but only received with a grateful and transformed heart. All of our experiences along the pilgrimage are used to change us closer and closer into the image of the beloved Son, with whom the Spirit makes us joint heirs of the Father.

One of the great blessings of living in a society that is changing so rapidly, constantly forcing us to be on the move, is that desettlement keeps us off balance and prevents us from attaching ourselves too closely to what Dante calls "secondary goods." The great job, the beautiful house, the loving parents who raised us, are at their very best secondary reflections of the love that has its source in God. The point is not to become preoccupied with the reflection but to turn and behold the One whom it reflects.

It isn't the next place that will somehow change the nomad into the man or woman they prefer to be, if they even have an idea of who that is. It is the love of God that can be found anyplace. And to grow in this love means that we have to keep leaving behind all of the old illusions that made us worship some part of creation rather than the Creator who made the current place, the last place, or next place so desirable.

Until we have turned our faces toward this loving God, we will never be able to love others authentically, because to love others requires that we give ourselves to them. And without receiving love from the primal Lover, there is no self of worth to give away in love. Conversely, having found this love from God, if we hoard it for ourselves we violate the nature of the Trinitarian love from which our self-worth is derived. In doing so the self loses its worth and even itself. Loving is at the core of our created being, and without the giving of ourselves to others we disappear into nonbeing.

In Ovid's famous poem about Narcissus we are introduced to a young man who was so beautiful that all of the nymphs loved him. Especially Echo, who could only repeat the last words she heard. But Narcissus was incapable of loving anyone. When he saw Echo, who loved him so desperately, he said, "I will die before I give you power over me." Tragically she echoed, "I give you power over me," and disappeared forever into a cave.

Then Narcissus saw his own reflection in a pool of water and fell in love for the first time. Not recognizing his own image, he keeps reaching into the pool, only to lose the new image. "Nor knows he who it is his arms pursue with eager clasps, but loves he knows not who." The redemptive message in this tragic poem is that until we find a new image of ourselves, we will never be able to love another. Either we will keep spurning love like Narcissus, or like Echo, we will give too much power to others until we disappear as persons. That is because we are looking for something in the other person that can only come from God, namely, the discovery that we are already cherished creatures.

When Narcissus stands up and realizes that the person he loves is himself, he says, "What I long for I have." Then he faces a great choice. He could return to the world free to authentically love and give himself away. But instead he returns to the pool and lies there consumed by his own image, until weak and spent he descends into the underworld.

Nomadic behavior is always narcissistic unless we make the other choice of giving away the self we long to love. The reason nomads wear out so many relationships is not because they are not interested in love, but because they have no cherished self to give to others. Since love was woven into our creation, without it the nomads are searching not only for love but for their very being. The belief that we are cherishable can come only from the source—the Creator who in Christ was dying to love us. To know this authentic love is inevitably to turn from our own reflection toward others. Then our nomadic journey is transformed from the search for a lovable self into a pilgrimage in which we are now searching only for ways to love as we have been loved.

THE BLESSING OF EMOTION

Love is inherently emotional, which did not originally refer to feelings, but to movement or a change of positions. To love someone is to move your life toward them and to leave the former position in which you were settled as an isolated individual. This emotion changes not only your settled position but your life as you move closer and closer toward intimacy with the other. And when do lovers ever move close enough? Never. It is always possible to experience more life-transforming motion toward the other, and true love will never settle for close enough. The possibility for deeper intimacy is as limitless as the Triune God from whose image this yearning is derived.

So to live in such an emotional society is not necessarily bad. It all depends on where and why we are moving. If the constant change of positions is only about finding ourselves, then it is both narcissistic and idolatrous. But if we have already found life's value in the love of God, then all of the social movement into which our lives are caught up is nothing more or less than opportunities for the missional activity of moving toward others with love.

In the name of Father, Son, and Spirit, you can love your neighbor in this town and in the next one to which you will be moving. You can love the new boss who is changing everything in the office, and the housekeeper and child-care provider you have to hire because that boss is keeping you away from home. Or you can choose to leave your job and stay with your children because you decide that is more loving, in spite of all the disruption it will cause to your family's lifestyle. What is normative in the Scriptures is not that we stay here or go there, work or be domestic, but that we glorify the Triune God by authentic and sacrificial acts of sacred love. It isn't at all clear from the Bible how we must give our lives away, but it is painfully clear that we can never get life just right and then settle down.

Even when we remain in community and relationships, we are never remaining in the same place we were yesterday. These relationships have a dynamic life that is always in motion, and thus always changing, for better or worse. The emotion is inevitable. It falls to our stewardship of them to decide if we will be moving closer or farther away, but only God is changeless. Everything else is within the Primum Mobile, which means it is in constant flux. Even our love for God is emotional in that we are moving toward him or looking back.

To love is to be in movement, which means both moving away from something preferred as well as moving toward the new objects of the compassion of God. And along the way, we discover that we are also moving closer to the God who in Jesus Christ left the preferred place of heaven to move toward us.

The most important reason to take the emotional society seriously is because God loves movement. When Dante's pilgrim saw the Primum Mobile, he described it as "The regal mantle folding itself round the turning spheres, and nearest to the breath and ways of God it burns and quickens most."[6] His point is that God created all of the movement. That is because it forces us to stay in motion, which is the only way we love, and thus, know God on our way home to him. However, it is striking that in the Empyrean, where God is found in perfect communion with the souls he has brought all the way home, there is no motion. Only perfect peace. The yearning to stop, which both nomads and pilgrims know, is finally satisfied. But not until we are really home. Even then, eternity is spent in full communion with the Triune Family, which is something that is never satiated. In the meantime our lives exist within the Primum Mobile, or the primal emotion, created by the Love calling us to that home.

THE BLESSING OF TRANSFORMATION

In the first canto of the poems of *Paradise*, Dante makes it clear that the closer we get to God, the more we change. This isn't a change into being an angelic being, a superhuman being, or even a different being, but a purer form of ourselves, which means that heaven is the place where we get back to being ourselves, and for some of us that means meeting a stranger.

Dante has a hard time describing what it means to change and yet become more the same. So he invents a word. "Transhumanize—it cannot be explained per verba [by words] so let this example serve until

God's grace grants the experience."[7] The prefix "trans" means across or movement, and "humanize" means to make more human. Thus, the closer we move to God the more human we become, which is one of the greatest mercies that is waiting at the end of the journey. When we are in full communion with God we can only be what he has made of us.

Here Dante is again working out of the Thomistic theological system, paramount in medieval thinking, that included the belief that grace does not destroy human nature but perfects it. And along the way we are brought closer and closer to God.

While Luther and Calvin had some misgivings about the implications of Aquinas's doctrine, they would have agreed that the goal of our sanctification is the restoration of God's righteous creation of our lives. But they would emphasize how this restoration occurs only in Jesus Christ. To live in Christ does not mean simply to act like Jesus, or to ask ourselves "What would Jesus do?" in a particular situation. Rather it means to be changed by the Spirit into his image—which is the real us. If we want to see the finished goal of all the transhumanizing activity that occurs in our lives on the pilgrimage home, we have only to look at the beloved Son of the Father. This does not erase or negate our individuality, but it does free us to be the created essence of ourselves, which is exactly what we were hoping to find when we were nomads roaming from place to place, job to job, and relationship to relationship. We were looking for ourselves. That is who the Spirit gives us when he changes us into the image of the Son.

This is why Paul's letters provide a constant invitation to live in Christ. We have a hard time understanding this because we have been nurtured in individualistic values for a long time. We consider it a right, if not a responsibility, to live our own lives. But in ancient society people attempted to live the life of someone who had gone before them. This is what the Ephesians were doing in the temple of Artemis, the Romans at the Areopagus, and throughout the Empire with their many mystery cults. It is what the Jews were accustomed to doing in their synagogues, where they told the stories of the patriarchs, kings, and prophets. They were living vicariously. When Jesus asked his disciples, "Who do people say that I am?" they responded by saying, "Some say Elijah, or John, or Jeremiah." The people knew these prophets were dead, but they thought Jesus was trying to follow the old practice of living in one of their great lives.

Paul is appealing to this common religious agenda by calling us to live the life of Jesus Christ. That is the movement, or emotion, of the Holy Spirit in our lives—to engraft us into Jesus' identity.

"Your life," Paul would tell us, "has already been lived." Your decisions have already been made. Your calling has already been given. Your morality has already been determined. And best of all your identity has already been established. You are no longer lost nomads. The Holy Spirit has adopted you into the Son's relationship with the Father, so that you are now the beloved of the Father. And he loves all of you. Not just the good parts. That is because Jesus Christ has embraced and redeemed it all. So that with Paul you can say, "It is no longer I who live, but Christ who lives in me."[8]

It is significant that while Lucifer was presented at the bottom of the "kingdom of all grief" as a giant, God is presented at the center of the "kingdom of all joy" as pure light.[9] Grief comes when we try to make ourselves large, and joy comes when the light of the Creator reveals his created goodness in our lives.

At the poems of *Paradise* progress, it gets harder and harder for the pilgrim to describe what he is seeing. He resorts to even more analogical language. He leaves behind the physical realm of dark woods, paths, mountain, and rivers, and enters into a realm of light, dance, and music. He uses fewer nouns and more verbs. Perhaps he is telling us that the essence of a human being is more verb than noun. In Christ, we are more about loving, giving, and worshiping than anything else. We just got a little confused about this when we were pretending to be nouns, like nomads.

THE BLESSING OF BEAUTY

Closely related to the blessing of transformation is the blessing of discovering God's beauty in all creation, including ourselves. The blessing is not simply in beholding the beauty, but in seeing it as a reflection that guides us home to the beauty of God.

The pilgrim notices that the closer Beatrice gets to God, the more beautiful she becomes. This is because the light of God reflects more strongly in her eyes. Near the end of his pilgrimage he tries to describe how a beautiful woman could become even more lovely, and then realizes that not only will his words fail this task but also that her beauty is now so overwhelming that his eyes cannot receive it all. "The beauty I saw there goes far beyond all mortal reach; I think that only He who made it knows the full joy of its being."[10] Such is the mark of true beauty. There is something more to it than we can ever grasp. That something is "He who made it."

The source of Beatrice's beauty is the reflection of God, in whose image she was made, and Christ, in whom she was restored. But as this restoration is revealed, she is clearly looking more and more like Beatrice, and even more herself than the pilgrim has ever seen before. His last vision of her is as she is seated in the Empyrean beholding her God. The great light that reflected off her face allowed the pilgrim finally to see the essence of her, and not as a reflection of his own projections, "for her image came down to be unblurred by anything."[11] In this moment he is finally able to move from infatuation to authentic love for her. We can only love authentically when the light of truth allows us to see others for who they really are—not what we want them to be, or what they want themselves to be, and certainly not what they pretended to be along the nomadic meandering through life when they were lost. Others are what God created them to be, and as we see this revealed we are able to really know them, and only then really love them. So eternity is spent not just being human, but in finally being the appreciated human.

Dante also recognizes others in paradise, but only as the beautiful essence of themselves, not as feeble or diseased. That is because they are now reflecting the light of God's glory. We tend to think that beauty comes from make-up that covers up the spots and wrinkles. In heaven, just the opposite is true—beauty is revealed by getting closer and closer to brilliant light. Thus, in the end we see that all of the exhortations to give God glory were not meant to diminish us, but finally to see the beauty of God's creativity in our lives as they reflect that glory.

Not only do human creatures reflect the beauty of God, but so does all creation. For Dante, the beauty of creation is found not in its inherent splendor, but in its order. "Among all things, however disparate, there reigns an order, and this gives the form that makes the universe resemble God . . . and in this order all created things, according to their bent, maintain their place, disposed in proper distance from their Source."[12] The squirrel reflects the beauty of God by running around collecting nuts, not by trying to be an elephant. The moon isn't the sun, and it glorifies

God only by staying in its place between the earth and sun. Humans reflect God's beauty only by being as human as possible.

The further the pilgrim travels on his journey through paradise, the more removed he becomes from the forms of creation, moving now in the realm of love and light that lies behind these forms and give them their beauty.[13] The significance of Dante's insight is that creation's beauty is best seen at the proper distance from its Source. Anyone who has stood in front of a beautiful painting understands this. Sometimes it's necessary to stand back in order to take the beauty in. So distance from God isn't necessarily bad, as long as we are continuing to reflect the sacred love with which we were created, to the capacity we have been given. In the words of Alister McGrath, "spiritual reality has to be accommodated to our capacity to handle it."[15] Otherwise, he claims, we would be staring at the sun.

As Dante's pilgrim eventually discovered, at the end of our journey we will have been transformed to the point that we can indeed look into the Light that gives light to the sun. But for those of us who are still on the pilgrimage through this life, it is enough to reflect that light from a distance to the capacity we have each been given. From the perspective of heaven, our beauty is directly related to accepting both the possibilities and limits of this capacity.

THE BLESSING OF PREDESTINATION

This doctrine, which claims that our eternity has been predestined by God, did not begin with John Calvin, but was articulated by Augustine before him, and by Paul before both of them. It is a difficult theology to accept, but it is particularly troubling to equality-minded nomads who feel they should all be given the same chance to end up in the right place. Given their resolve to find that place on their own, the real offense of the doctrine for nomads is not that some may be predestined to hell, but that even if they were predestined to heaven it would mean they got there only by grace.

Down through the church's history the doctrine of predestination has dragged behind it some heavy theological baggage that tries to reconcile God's complete sovereignty with his gift of freedom to humanity. Since the Bible itself simply affirms both claims, it is possible to accept both predestination and free will even if they can't be reconciled logically.[15] As Virgil would say, reason will only get us so far. We make further progress on the journey simply by following the revelation we have received.

Dante's interest in the doctrine is not to account for why some are in heaven and others in hell, but to understand the inequities among the saintly visions. What he wants to understand is why everyone doesn't have the same extraordinary visions that mystics and saints enjoy. The reason this is so important is because our eternal joy, as well as our joy along the way home, is determined by our vision of God.

As depicted in *Paradise,* it is clear that even in heaven not everyone is equally blessed. That's because the bestowal of blessings comes only as a grace from God. Depending on the amount of grace given through predestination, people have different capacities for visions of God. But since everyone is enjoying God to their full capacity, they are all perfectly joyful. While all of the souls are actually at home with God in Empyrean, the highest heaven, the pilgrim sees their reflections in the various nine spheres he ascends along the way. This is to distinguish their measure of grace from God.

When the pilgrim is passing through the lowest sphere, he asks a woman why she can be content with such a low place in the eternal scheme. "But tell me all you souls so happy here, do you not yearn for a higher post in Heaven, to see more, to become more loved by Him?" Notice the repeated use of the word more. As one of Dante's biographers has written, it has "almost an American ring."[16]

The woman gently smiles at the pilgrim and then says, "Brother, the virtue of our heavenly love tempers our will and makes us want no more than what we have—we thirst for this alone. . . . His will is our peace."

This is the line the clears up the confusion for the pilgrim. In response he says, "Then it was clear to me that every where of Heaven is Paradise, though there the light of Grace Supreme does not shine equally."[17]

The inferno may have been all about climbing down, and purgatory about climbing up, but no one in paradise is trying to climb anymore. "His will is our peace." This means that peace and blessings come not from wanting more and more, but from finding our place in the will of God. That's pretty prophetic thinking for a society that keeps telling us our happiness is dependent on improving ourselves. It's the lure of this dream that keeps us moving from place to place. But it just never works. That is because it's the same old person who keeps moving to all of those new places.

Not only happiness, but a joyful peace comes from beholding God with whatever capacity we have been given. The goal isn't to increase our capacity, but to fill up the potential that typically lies dormant. When we make that our focus, we have already entered paradise, which by definition is the place where we finally aren't addicted to wanting more. And that is precisely why predestination is a blessing for the nomad.

THE BLESSING OF VISION

When Beatrice has finished bringing the pilgrim back to God she ceases to serve as his guide. Like Virgil, who represented truth, she who represents the grace of God can only take the pilgrim so far. Grace takes us further than reason, but even it is only a means to communion. Eventually the time comes for the pilgrim to commune and look directly into the light of God. For this he needs his final guide, Bernard of Clairvaux, a twelfth-century abbot who was renown for his sermons on the loving visions of God that enflame the soul.

Six hundred years before Bernard, another monastic named Benedict described the journey to God as climbing a ladder. The only way that progress is made up the ladder is through prayer and humility. Thus, we go up by bowing down. Bernard developed this doctrine by claiming that Benedict's ladder leads to perfect love and eternal light. When we get to the top of the ladder, it's time to enter the love and light. In describing heaven, Bernard used the image of King Solomon's banquet, a place of delight and joy where we rest in the king's tender embrace and see things that are invisible apart from his light.

In his *Sermons on the Song of Songs*, Bernard claimed that God is not so much perceived as vaguely felt and apprehended, and even that in a passing way and by the light of a sudden momentary blaze of glory, so that a great flame of love is enkindled in the soul.[18] Beholding this light gives us a subjective knowledge of God. With this knowledge comes what he termed a re-cognition. What begins with a recognition of God results in a re-cognition of our way of thinking.

When Bernard leads the pilgrim into the light of God, he is at first blinded by its glory. But he then recovers his vision to see nothing the same again. His perception of life and all things have been re-cognated. That's what a vision of our home with the Triune God provides. It is given not only for the joy and delight of being in the King's embrace, but in order to provide new vision for our life on the way to that home.

While the mystical stream has continued to flow through the Catholic tradition, many Protestants don't quite know what to make of it and often look with some envy on those who have seen heavenly visions that change everything. Luther and Calvin didn't search for mystical experiences, but neither did they repudiate them. They simply didn't think they were necessary. If we want to see what Bernard saw and what Dante described, they claimed, we have only to look at Jesus Christ. "So if you have been raised with Christ, seek the things that are above, where Christ is, seated at the right hand of God. Set your mind on things that are above, not on things that are on earth, for you have died and your life is hidden with Christ in God. When Christ who is your life is revealed, then you will also be revealed with him in glory."[19]

The reason we are called to set our minds on things that are above is not to ignore the things on earth, but to discover a sanctifying vision that allows us to become the love of God on earth. At the heart of this vision is the discovery that by the Spirit our life is found in the Son who is at the Father's right hand. When we have a re-cognition that this is our true home, we can then make a world of difference by living in Christ today. We are free, as Luther claimed, to be the little christ to the house of our neighbor.

As someone said to me at the conclusion of a worship service that was again focused on our life in Christ, "Jesus, Jesus, Jesus. It always gets back to Jesus."

And I who was approaching now the end
    off all man's yearning, strained with all of the force
    in me to raise my burning longing high.

Dante, *Paradise,* XXXIII. 46–48, p. 391

The End of Our Yearning

Communing with Home along the Way

I f a vision of the heavenly home is so critical to the pilgrimage of life, then the final question is, How will that vision be found? Given the nature of our nomadic society, it is no longer possible to inculcate that vision through settled communities; and given the nature of our souls, they could never settle into those places anyway. They are at home only with Father, Son, and Spirit. But we're a long way off from that home and are in dire need of some means of communication with it along the way.

That is exactly what Jesus left us in the sacrament that invites Holy Communion with the Triune God.

THE YEARNING FOR TRANSCENDENCE

When the twelfth century began, medieval Europe appeared to be coming apart at the seams. The old Holy Roman Empire was in chaos,

Muslim soldiers were invading from the East and had already taken half of Spain, the new monarchies were shaky and locked into constant conflict with Rome, and the church itself was badly in need of reform. A new economy based on tradesmen, merchants, and developing urban centers was beginning to undermine the familiar old ways of knights, peasants, and the medieval manor.[1]

In the midst of all this upheaval, at a quiet Benedictine monastery four miles north of Paris, a new *axis mundi* was being discovered that could tie the crumbling society to heaven. Abbot Suger had the audacity in such frightening times to launch a major new building program that would reconstruct his monastery church in St. Denis. He was even bold enough to try out a new architectural form that we now call Gothic.

The normative architectural form for churches prior to the twelfth century was a form borrowed from the Roman basilica, and thus called Romanesque. It was characterized by heavy, squatty walls and barrel vaults. Since the walls needed to be so massive to hold up the roof, the windows could not be large, nor could the construction be very high. The Romans used the basilica long before there was a church, and its original purpose was simply to be a public meeting place. When the church adopted this form, it placed the communion table near the apse where the Romans conducted official business, and placed the bishop in the seat behind the table where a magistrate used to sit. But the form was never designed to suggest transcendence, which was the missing ingredient Abbot Suger wanted to include in his renovations. Within a ten-year period Gothic cathedrals were also begun in Chartes and Sens. Eventually they spread throughout France, England, Germany, and Eastern Europe. But the church at St. Denis is cherished among historians of architecture because, as a renovation, it serves as the transitional form from Romanesque to Gothic, containing in one building both the old and the new.

In building the Gothic cathedral, Suger and his architects were creating a vision for the household of God on earth. To accomplish this, they borrowed from the experiments of the Normans with cross-ribbed vaults, developed the concept, and placed them on large pillars that could soar in height. Since the roof was held by these interior pillars, the walls could be thin, stabilizing their height with the beautiful exterior flying buttresses. Now it was possible to include large windows that allowed the sunlight to pour into the church. These large windows were not so much openings in the walls, as in Romanesque buildings, but were designed to give the impression that the walls themselves were transparent. Eventually other Gothic cathedrals added stained glass and Rosetta windows, but it was the pointed arches, towering height, geometric order, straight serene lines, and most of all the abundance of light that contributed to a new encounter with the transcendent God.

It is not surprising that the primary theological influence on Suger's renovations was Bernard of Clairvaux, whose visions depicting the light of the heavenly city were about to be written in stone. Drawing from Platonic writings, the medievalists had long believed that light was the most noble of natural phenomena, because it was the least material. This made it a more pure analogy of the divine light and love that binds all creation to its Creator. It was also Bernard's influence that convinced the new Gothic churches that all the figurative sculptures and paintings that had previously adorned the dark Romanesque walls were no longer necessary. The church itself was now a work of art. For Bernard, the purpose of religious art was not to be representational but symbolic, calling the beholder into the mystical reality that is symbolized. In other words, inviting us into union with God.

This means that the Gothic cathedral was never meant to be just a lovely building in which worship is conducted. It is rather the celestial city into which the worshiper enters. Some of our architectural historians have for this reason challenged the notion that Gothic was a logical sequel to Romanesque, and have claimed that we should rather see it as a competitor, "created as its emphatic antithesis."[2] It wasn't Roman but French, and it wasn't a house adapted for worship but a house of worship. Immediately upon walking in, one's head kicks back to look up, and the soul breathes sighs of awe and wonder that it has found a home away from home. When a people have found such a place where heaven has intersected with earth, they are renewed in the conviction that God is with them. And convinced of that, they can do the most amazing things—all as a way of affirming that they live on holy ground.

Although the twelfth century began in disarray, the introduction of Gothic architecture was only the beginning of a series of transformations that would leave the century as the high cultural mark of the middle ages. Over the next hundred years other revolutions followed in science, technology, politics, theology, and the literature of poets like Dante. By the close of the twelfth century, universities had been born, where further developments would be made in all of these areas. While it would be an overstatement to claim that the introduction of Gothic architecture was the cause of all these transformations, leading medievalists do consider it to be a critical symbol of the new era.[3] The French scholar M. D. Chenu has demonstrated that the cultural renaissance of the twelfth century began when its thinkers became renewed in the conviction that the universe was a sacred entity of which humanity was a part.[4] The Gothic cathedral was the window into that unity binding heaven and earth. When people are renewed in their vision of the heavenly home, they become creative again, striving to integrate the beauty of heaven into all of life.

The twenty-first century has also begun in a time of disarray, desettlement, and confusion. Many are tempted to despair. We in the West have achieved a quality of life for many that was beyond the furthest reaches of the medieval imagination, but that has only revealed the poverty of our souls. We know all too well how to make a good living but are clueless about how to make a good life.

We work extremely hard at life. But all of the long hours in the office, the relentless errands in the minivan, the collecting of more junk to stuff into our houses, and the crazed nomadic search to find a better place to do it all just isn't working. Many would claim that life isn't all that bad for them, but just a little frayed around the edges. But when even a single thread of life starts to pull apart, it isn't long before the rest of it unravels as well. When an overstressed child becomes dark and depressed, a job is lost, or a marriage loses its intimacy, it soon feels like all of life is chaotic and falling apart. It isn't difficult to get people to admit that their souls are already in disarray.

That is why so many have been turning to spirituality in recent years. They know their world has somehow come unhinged from heaven, and they are desperately looking for a way to reconnect it. But they aren't flocking into the neo-Gothic churches that typically stand as tired dinosaurs in the middle of the communities that have themselves become anything but a community.

In his book *After Heaven: Spirituality in America Since the 1950s,* Robert Wuthnow has traced the change in Western religious life from being dwelling oriented to seeker oriented. As he states, "dwelling-oriented spirituality has become increasingly difficult to sustain because complex social realities leave many Americans with a sense of spiritual homelessness. Seeking-oriented spirituality requires individuals to negotiate their own understandings and experiences of the sacred."[5] Typical of the seeker-oriented spirituality is the extremely popular book by Thomas Moore called *Care of the Soul: A Guide for Cultivating Depth and Sacredness in Everyday Life*. Utilizing a "psychological polytheism," Moore advocates the necessity of finding small truths in many places, rather than deriving our vision of life from a single religious source.[6] This allows us, he believes, to participate in the messy confusion of pluralistic life freed from the old notions of finding a single integrating source, which is exactly what home used to offer us. Even with all of these sources of insight, Moore claims that it is necessary to move beyond the idea that the soul can be saved from any of the transcendent sources. That is because "dropping the salvational fantasy frees us up to the possibility of self knowledge and self acceptance."[7] As Wuthnow points out, this new attention being placed on the soul isn't really about the soul at all, which Moore refuses to define. It is rather a further development of the fascination we had with the "inner self" in previous decades.

In spite of the attraction we have to these new seeker-oriented spiritualities, any effort to find salvation from self-knowledge and acceptance is not going to resolve the deep angst that persists in the alienated soul. It's the self that's the problem. To attempt an a la carte collection of small truths from various religious systems, ranging from Buddhism to witchcraft, all in the effort to rebuild the self, will only internalize the messy confusion, which is what is tearing at the soul. The soul belongs to God. It was created by him, for him, and will only be at home in him. Thus, the soul by definition is a yearning for God.

What is needed today is exactly the same thing that was needed in the early twelfth century and every century from the time Cain was cursed to wander the earth. The soul is longing for its lost paradise where we were at home with our Creator. As Dante states, that is the end of all our yearning, and we will never be satisfied with less than at least a glimpse of this transcendent home along the way. Thus, the challenge is to find today what the introduction of Gothic offered medieval society—a place along the way where the vision of heaven is renewed.

THE YEARNING FOR A WAY

A generation before the introduction of the Gothic cathedral, another revolution was transpiring in the theological realm. In 1098, St. Anselm of Canterbury published a new doctrine of the atonement in his treatise *Cur Deus Homo,* or *Why Did God Become Human?* The purpose of this treatise was to stress the unique work of Jesus Christ in providing a satisfactory sacrifice for our sins. Anselm had struggled with the justice of God, wanting to know how a just God could offer salvation to those whose sin of corrupting themselves and the world merited only death. He knew that God was merciful, but he also knew that God's mercy had to be consistent with his justice. Thus, his forgiveness had to involve more than simply annulling our sins. He resolved this dilemma by claiming that God is just not because he rewards according to merit, but because he does what is most appropriate to himself, which is the highest good. Thus, only God can satisfy God, which is exactly what he does in the sacrifice of Jesus Christ on the cross.

The significance of this breakthrough is that it created a dramatic shift away from the old penitential system that was dominated by the monastics. The way the old system worked was that monks, who had dedicated their lives to prayer, were expected to pray for the sins of the world. Eventually this digressed into praying for the penance of the patrons of the monastery. But Anselm's claim that only the sacrifice of Christ can provide satisfaction for our sins began to win a broad acceptance in the church. This shifted the *axis mundi* away from the monastic chamber, where a monk struggled for penance, toward the Mass, where a priest stood behind the altar declaring the sacrifice of Christ. And it all happened right about the time Suger and the architects of Gothic were giving us a new vision of the heavenly city on earth—with a high altar.

When Dante began *The Divine Comedy* at the beginning of the 1300s, he was steeped in all of this. Not only does his vision of paradise utilize all of Bernard's symbols of light and love, but he also adopts his use of symbol as a means to enter mystical union with God. Dante's entire poetry is a cathedral of mystical symbols. But so does he give evidence of the pervasive influence of Anselm. As he depicts Beatrice leading the pilgrim through paradise, at one point she explains, "Your nature, when it sinned once and for all in its first root, was exiled from these honors, as it was dispossessed of Paradise; nor could man recover what was lost. . . ."[8] Then she said that since humanity was unable to make amends with "obedience too late," it remained for God in his own ways "to bring man back to integrity." So then, she continued,

> "Between that final night and the first day
>   no act so lofty, so magnificent
>   was there, or shall there be, by either way
>
> for God, Who gave Himself, gave even more
>   so that mankind might raise itself again
>   than if He simply annulled the debt;
>
> and other means would have been less
>   than Justice, if God's only Son had not
>   humbled himself to take on mortal flesh."[9]

If the end of our yearning is for the transcendent paradise, it only follows that the way to get there must come from heaven toward earth because it is the nature of transcendence to be inaccessible to mortals. Especially alienated mortals. That way is God's only Son.

None of God's acts are "so lofty, so magnificent" as the incarnation and sacrifice of Christ, because it is God's means of returning our alienated souls to himself. Since this mercy flows out of God's highest good, it is an act of justice to God by God. Our hope to rise up again into communion with God is found not in our penance, and certainly not in our desperate attempts at self-acceptance, but only through this grace of God. Everything else fails the test of divine justice. And in our souls we know it.

The reason the nomads work so hard at life is because they really are trying to get it right. The commitment to justice is written on their souls, which is why they knock themselves out to build a life that truly rises up to something. But it is this same sense of justice that condemns all of their efforts, because they are their worst critics. No matter where they go, or what they try next, it is never good enough. About that, at least, they are correct. When they stumble into a church and hear the preacher speak about the grace of God, they just glaze over with confusion. "Well, that's not right," I often hear, but what they really mean is that it isn't justice.

God raises us up through the sacrifice of Christ because it is just to his own nature to be merciful. As Beatrice explains, "the deed gratifies more the doer . . . it manifests the innate goodness of the good heart from which it springs."[10] Grace isn't God doing right by us, but by God. Why? Only because he's the Father who wants his lost children to come back home. And he won't wait for death to get us, but offers a way to commune with our transcendent home along the journey of life, that we may have life.

To understand the significance of this sacrifice of Christ as our way is to hunger for the same thing the twelfth-century church did—communion with the means of grace.

THE YEARNING FOR COMMUNION

Anselm's sacrificial theology continues to guide the teachings and affections of the Catholic church.[11] The call to personal penance was maintained, but not as a means of atoning for our sins, and certainly not as a means of atoning for the sins of others. In addition to the ongoing monastic life of prayer, the Catholics have also benefited richly from the scholastic theology of Aquinas, the mystical traditions, and renewal and missionary movements such as those of the Dominicans, Franciscans, and later the Jesuits. They have also been guided by the leadership of the popes, who often led extremely significant reform movements in their service as the vicar of Christ for the church. In more recent years, the tradition has become as diverse as every other religious tradition, with emphases as divergent as the radical liberation theologians to those who believe Mary should be elevated to a member of the Godhead. But the heart of the Catholic tradition has continued to be devoted to the altar where the Mass is celebrated, the body of Christ is sacrificed, and the faithful receive heaven's means of grace.

When the Protestant Reformation began to sweep through some parts of Europe in the sixteenth century, one of the regular points of debate was over what exactly happens at the altar to make it a means of grace. Not only did Martin Luther and John Calvin debate the Catholics, but they also debated each other and other Protestants. Luther's emphasis was not on the repeated sacrifice, but on the Word of God that was made visible in communion and conjoined with the bread and wine. Using the analogy of the incarnation, he claimed that the finite can bear the infinite. Though rejecting the Catholic doctrine of transubstantiation, which claimed that the bread and wine become literally the body and blood of Christ, Luther did continue to maintain the corporeal presence of Christ in, with, under, around, and behind the altar.

Calvin rejected the whole notion of an altar, and replaced it with a table, in the tradition of the early church. He also claimed that the sacrament was a means of revealing the transcendent grace of God, but he did not want to physically locate Christ in the elements of bread and wine. Christ, he claimed, is present at the right hand of the Father as well as in the hearts of the communicants. It is the Holy Spirit who meets us at the table and lifts us to our adopted place in the Triune communion. In the process we experience the miraculous exchange of our sins for Christ's righteousness. Thus, what gets converted in the sacrament is not the elements but the communicants. Like Luther, Calvin also tied the sacrament to the Word

Other Protestants, such as Zwingli, thought that the emphasis should not be on what Christ does in the sacrament, but on the pledging of the church to remember and trust in the atonement of Christ. He distrusted the notion of a physical means of grace. As Zwingli claimed, nothing can mediate God but God, for salvation is not found in Christ eaten but in Christ crucified. Many of the Anabaptists took it a step further, rejecting the whole concept of a sacrament and believing that communion was a sign of grace already given to believers.

As this brief survey of fifteenth-century continental debates over the sacrament reveals, the churches' divergent theologies of communion have kept them separated. Most of the various twenty-first century churches can trace their understanding of communion to one of these traditions, and for that reason, among others, they have remained separated. It would be possible to cynically denounce the churches for dividing the body of Christ over a meal he instituted for our unity, but the reasons for the debate about communion are central to the very identity of these churches and to their various understandings of how we receive the grace that comes from the heavenly home into our souls.

All of the churches agree, however, that it is only by grace that we have any opportunity to commune with Father, Son, and Spirit. It is God's just and merciful way for us to enter into the cathedral of light as we progress on our pilgrimage home. And they agree that we need to commune with this means of grace if we are ever going to find our way to the end of the soul's yearning for God.

Whether they realize it or not, nomads are searching for a place to commune with something beyond themselves. Their souls are worn out from constantly looking to the next place, the next relationship, or the next job for their salvation. And after swallowing too many introspective therapies and self-awareness books, they're becoming convinced that when they look deep within themselves they find nothing. They are tired of the hustle, tired of the illusions, and tired of themselves. As all of the fascination today in anything spiritual reveals, the vague memory of the Father's house is returning to those who feel spent and are dismayed at how life has turned out. Even an empty soul knows it was created for something more.

If the church does not offer these nomads a means of communing with transcendent holiness, they will continue to shop their way through the spiritual fad du jour. But the yearning is not a fad. It is as old as Cain, and it's not going away anytime soon. What will ultimately transform the nomads into pilgrims is not the church's many programs tailored to address felt needs, for that just reduces the body of Christ to one more provider of what Dante called "secondary goods," and it continues to enslave the nomad in the identity of being a consumer. It is time for the churches to stop developing their evangelism strategies from marketing experts, and to speak from the defining core of our existence, namely, that we have a means to commune with holiness. For the yearning to find these two things is at the defining core of the nomad: transcendence and communion.

Every church from Catholic to Mennonite knows how to offer these two things. It is what both unites us and distinguishes us, because it is at the core of our identity. The distinctives aren't the problem for either nomads or pilgrims. This is not to diminish the significance of our theological differences about what is happening at the altar, or even if it should be a table, or whether we best call it Mass, Eucharist, Communion, or the Lord's Supper. But clearly most churches have progressed to the point where they no longer say it is impossible to be a Christian unless you're a member of their church. Implicit in the recognition of faith beyond our denominational identities is the affirmation that other churches also have a legitimate means of grace, a proclamation that the sacrifice of Jesus is heaven's way for us to come home, and in Christ we can experience Triune communion today.

This is not to suggest the only thing the church needs to be doing today is to administer the sacrament of Communion. Every church has at least one other sacrament, such as baptism, even if they don't call it a sacrament. And they all have at least one other mark that defines their existence, such as the proclamation of God's Word. The ministry of the church, of course, needs to include opportunities for congregational care, fellowship, mission, and biblical study. But when these ministries lose as their reason for existence to support, inform, or manifest our communion with the transcendent God, they become only distractions to the soul and competitors for its affection. We come to the church not to have a therapeutic, social, activist, or educational experience, but to have a communal experience as the household of God with the Father, Son, and Spirit. The means Jesus instituted to convey this grace, and the means the early church used every week to be strengthened in this grace, was the sacrament of Holy Communion.

If the nomads are going to be invited into the communion enjoyed by the household of God, then they dare not be kept strangers and aliens to the grace we proclaim. This means the sacrament must be made accessible to those who are both liturgically and biblically illiterate. That doesn't mean that we simply throw a few praise songs into the worship. It means that the whole notion of worship has to be built around entering into holiness and finding communion with it. This has nothing to do with the dynamism of the music or the profound insights of the preacher and everything to do with Suger's vision to build a place of worship where the head goes up, the knees go down, and the soul leaps up to rejoice in being finally home.

In a nomadic, seeker-oriented society we are not going to be able to depend on our buildings to do that for us. It has to be accomplished by the worship service itself. It doesn't matter if the church gathers in an old cathedral or the rented gymnasium of the local elementary school. What matters is transcendence and communion.

Accessibility also means that the churches have to get over the notion that God's holiness is in need of protection and can only be offered to those who know the right theological formulas. As St. Augustine explained, a sacrament cannot be contaminated, because its holiness is not found in the celebrant or the communicant, but in the Christ. Nobody comes to the table or altar because they deserve to be there, least of all those who have deluded themselves into self-righteousness. We all come only because we need to be there, and by grace the way has been unfolded from heaven's shores into our congregations.

Finally, the notion of making communion accessible means that it must make God accessible as well. The celebration of the sacrament is not about the liturgy or the fine silver that was donated by someone's grandfather. It is not about the church or our debated means of administering it, and it is certainly not about those who come to it frequently missing the significance of what is being offered. It is only about God's grace. That grace is not limited by the means of administration, the theology we express about the sacrament, or even the sins we bring to it. The sacrament calls us to place our eyes on something holier than ourselves. It is impossible to make it all about you. This is why it is so healing to the self-saturated nomad who is dying to find a home in something greater than the self. No one can approach the broken body of Christ and still nurture the identity of being a victim. Nor can anyone approach poured out blood and pride themselves on how hard they are working. And no one who is paying attention can leave the sacrament without remembering that they belong to a Triune family.

YEARNING FOR THE STARS

The three books of Dante's *Divine Comedy* all end with visions of the stars. At the end of the *Inferno* the pilgrim sees them above him. At the end of *Purgatory* he has climbed up to them, and at the end of *Paradise* he has entered into the love that moves them. These stars guide his journey home until he has finally found his place with the loving Triune circle. They provide just enough light along the way, until he can enter the light.

In addition to needing transcendence and communion along the way, pilgrims also need to believe that their journey really will end in the heavenly stars. There was a day when the church was accused of being so heavenly minded that we were no earthly good, but it would be pretty hard to make that charge stick today. Now preachers knock themselves out to be contextual and relevant to the pressing issues of daily life. Ironically, they are trying so hard to relate to a culture in which the nomad has lost interest. As the apostle said, "If for this life only we have hoped in Christ, we are of all people most to be pitied."[12] Unless we truly believe there is a place called heaven, we don't have any business trying to commune with it along the way.

This book has been all about the difference it makes in our life on earth if we believe that our home is in heaven. But all of this assumes that we really do believe. I believe. I believe that it is so much more than a symbol or an Archimedean perspective from which to analyze our nomadic meanderings. I believe that there is a real place called heaven, which is more real than anything on earth.

The Bible actually gives us very little information about heaven, except a few metaphors and symbols which, like Dante's *Divine Comedy*, serve as means for inspiring our life on earth. That's because the Bible wasn't written to describe paradise for us, but to be God's Word for the pilgrimage on the way there. The most important thing the Bible says about heaven is that it exists, and that it is the place where we will exist with God for eternity. But before heaven is a place, it is first of all a relationship with God, or perhaps an eternal place in the heart of God. Bernard would tell us that it's even better than relationship, it is union with God, and those who experience that find the sacred union with all things. Dante adds that when we are in union with God we are "impelled" by his love, which means that even in heaven we will continue to move. Only now it's the movement as "partners in a dance who whirl in their reel." And the best part is that this celestial dance is with "the One and Two and Three who forever reign as the Three and Two and One."[13]

One thing is certain from the Bible—heaven is home. And it will be good to finally arrive at home.

These days, every time I have Communion I think about my Dad being in heaven, and I rejoice that our communion is not only with God but with all of the saints whose pilgrimage on earth is done. In some important ways, I feel closer to my father now than I ever did when he was alive, which was pretty much Bernard's point. I often even say a quiet prayer of eucharistic gratitude that he is no longer lost as the nomad who's just wandering around through life. The sacrifice of Christ has made a way home for all who sacrificed their own lives trying to get to the wrong places. By grace, we are brought back to where we always belonged. To paradise.

> At this point power failed high fantasy
>   but like a wheel in perfect balance turning.
>   I felt my will and my desire impelled
>
> by the Love that moves the sun and the other stars.[14]

Notes

CHAPTER 1

1. Dante Alighieri, *The Divine Comedy: Volume 1, The Inferno*, trans. Mark Musa (New York: Penguin, 1984).

2. See chapter four, "Chasing the Lie," in M. Craig Barnes, *Yearning* (Downers Grove, Ill.: InterVarsity Press, 1991), pp. 67–85.

3. U. S. Census Bureau, "General Mobility By Region, Sex, and Age," *Current Population Survey*, March 2000.

4. Deborah Tall, *From Where We Stand: Recovering a Sense of Place* (New York: Knopf, 1993), p. 89.

5. David Sopher, "The Landscape of Home: Myth, Experience, Social Meaning," in D.W. Mening, ed. *The Interpretation of Ordinary Landscapes: Geographical Essays* (New York: Oxford University Press, 1979), p. 134.

6. Francis Mayes, *Under the Tuscan Sun: At Home in Italy* (New York: Broadway Books, 1996), p. 147.

7. See especially: James Howard Kunstler, *The Geography of Nowhere* (New York: Simon and Schuster, 1993); Ray Oldenburg, *The Great Good Place* (New York: Paragon House, 1990); Gary Paul Nabhah and Stephen Trimble, *The Geography of Childhood* (Boston: Beacon Press, 1994); Deborah Tall, *From Where We Stand: Recovering a Sense of Place* (New York: Knopf, 1993); Maggie Jackson, *What's Happening to Home? Balancing Life, Work, and Refuge in the Information Age* (Notre Dame, Ind.: Sorin Books, 2002).

8. Gary Pindell, *A Good Place to Live: America's Last Migration* (New York: Henry Holt, 1995), p. 2.

9. Dante, *Inferno*, p. 67.

10. Dante, *Inferno*, p. 67.

CHAPTER 2

1. T. S. Elliot, *Four Quartets* (New York: Harcourt, Brace, and Co., 1943), "Burnt Norton," II, lines 16 and 19.

2. Paul Ricoeur, "Biblical Hermeneutics," *Semeia* 4 (1975): 33–34, 122–28.

3. Mircea Eliade, *The Sacred & The Profane: The Nature of Religion* (New York: Harcourt Brace Jovanovich, 1959), pp. 33–36.

4. Joseph Campbell, *Historical Atlas of World Mythology,* vol. II (New York: Harper and Row, 1989), p. 154.

5. Dante, *Inferno,* V.121–23, p. 113.

6. Dante, *Inferno,* II.70, p. 81.

7. Genesis 12:1–2.

8. Jeremiah 29:7.

9. Dante, *Inferno,* III.34–49, p. 90.

10. *The Rule of St. Benedict,* Timothy Fry, OSB, ed. (Collegeville, Minn.: Liturgical Press, 1981), p. 171.

11. John Barth, *The Floating Opera* (New York: Bantam, 1956), p. 7.

12. Luke 13:29.

CHAPTER 3

1. Dante Alighieri, *La Vita Nuova,* trans. Mark Musa (New York: Oxford University Press, 1992).

2. Mark Musa, "Introduction," in *Inferno,* p. 26.

3. James W. Michaels, "Oh, Our Aching Angst," *Forbes* 150:6, (14 September 1992), p. 47.

4. Lyrics by Samuel Fillmore Bennett, music by Joseph Philbrick Webster (Boston: O. Ditson Publishing Co., 1868).

5. Walter Brueggemann, *Hope Within History* (Atlanta: John Knox, 1987), p. 80.

6. Roger Finke and Rodney Stark, *The Churching of America, 1776-1990: Winners and Losers in Our Religious Economy* (New Brunswick: Rutgers University Press, 1992), p. 15.

7. Mark A. Noll, *America's God: From Jonathan Edwards to Abraham Lincoln* (New York: Oxford University Press, 2002), p. 181.

8. Sidney E. Ahlstrom, *A Religious History of the American People* (New Haven: Yale University Press, 1973), p. 952.

9. Although the American Pledge of Allegiance was developed in 1892, the phrase, "one nation under God" was added by Congress in 1954.

10. See especially Reinhold Niebuhr, *The Nature and Destiny of Man: A Christian Interpretation* (Louisville: Westminster John Knox, 1996).

11. J. R. Baxter Jr., "This World Is Not My Home" (Dallas: Stamps-Baxter Music and Printing Company, 1946).

12. See James Howard Kunstler, *The Geography of Nowhere* (New York: Simon and Schuster, 1993). He painstakingly documents all of the mistakes the suburbs made, but he reserves his harshest criticism for the ways in which the automobile has dismantled the sense of a place for Americans.

13. Ray Oldenburg, *The Great Good Place* (New York: Paragon House, 1990).

14. Robert F. Kennedy, *To Seek a Newer World* (New York: Bantam, 1967), p. 53.

15. Pico Iver, "Stranger in a Strange Land," *Utne Reader* 100 (July–August 2000): p. 42.

16. Joan Osborne, "One of Us," from the album *Relish,* Eric Bazilian, music and lyrics (Los Angeles: Warner Bros., 1995).

CHAPTER 4

1. Peter Berger, Brigitte Berger, Hansfried Kellner, *The Homeless Mind: Modernization and Consciousness* (New York: Random House, 1973), p. 41.

2. Peter Berger, *The Sacred Canopy* (New York: Anchor, 1969), p. 107.

3. Kenneth J. Gergen, *The Saturated Self* (New York: Basic Books, 1991), p. 170.

4. Douglas Coupland, *Girlfriend in a Coma* (New York: Regan Books, 1998), p. 215.

5. Dietrich Bonhoeffer, *Life Together,* trans. John Doberstein, (New York: Harper & Row, 1954), pp. 26–27.

6. Athanasius, "On the Incarnation," *Library of Christian Classics,* vol. III, ed. Edward Roche Hardy (Philadelphia: Westminster, 1954), p. 57.

7. Gerald G. May, *The Awakened Heart: Opening Yourself to the Love You Need* (San Francisco: Harper San Francisco, 1993), p. 1.

8. Henri Frederic Amiel, *Amiel's Journal,* quoted in Alister McGrath, *The Unknown God: Searching for Spiritual Fulfillment* (Grand Rapids: Eerdmans, 1999), p. 114.

9. Zechariah 4:10.

10. Matthew 7:24–27.

11. Karl Barth, *Church Dogmatics* IV/2 (Edinburgh: T&T Clark, 1958), p. 565.

12. Simone Weil, *The Need for Roots: Prelude to a Declaration of Duties Toward Mankind,* trans. Arthur Willis (New York: G. P. Putnam's Sons, 1952; reprint, New York: Harper Colophon Books, 1971), p. 3.

13. W. S. Merwin, "Words From a Totem Animal," quoted in Frances Mayes, *Under the Tuscan Sun* (New York: Broadway Books, 1996), p. 147.

CHAPTER 5

1. Dante, *Inferno*, I.60, p. 69.
2. After writing the *Vita Nuova*, Dante's next major writing was the *Convivio*, which was his tribute to his second love, philosophy and reason. In *The Divine Comedy*, Dante developed the themes of both earlier works by weaving together the relationships of reason and love. Virgil, the embodiment of rationality, will guide the pilgrim toward his true passion until he arrives at the door of paradise, where only love can take him further. But even the guide of rationality is given as a loving grace from heaven to help him stay on the right path to the right place.
3. Dante, *Inferno*, I.91, p.70.
4. Karl Barth, *Church Dogmatics* IV/2, p. 560.
5. John Donne, *The Divine Poems*, ed. Helen Gardner (London: Oxford University Press, 1952), p. 51.
6. Dante, *Inferno*, XI.82, p. 170.
7. Dante, *Inferno*, XVII.121–36, p. 236.
8. Dante, *Inferno*, V.103–5, p. 112.
9. Dante, *Inferno*, VII.52–59, p. 131.
10. Dante, *Inferno*, XIII.151, p. 191.
11. Matthew 5:29–30.
12. Dante, *Inferno*, X.100-3, p. 161.
13. Richard Ford, *The Sportswriter* (New York: Vintage, 1995), p. 24.
14. Ford, *The Sportswriter*, p. 47.
15. John 10:9.
16. Dante, *Inferno*, III. 124–26, p. 93.
17. Dante, *Inferno*, XXXIV.334–36, p. 380.
18. Dante, *Inferno*, XXXIV. 136–39, p. 383.

CHAPTER 6

1. Dante Alighieri, *The Divine Comedy: Volume II, Purgatory*, trans. Mark Musa (New York: Penguin, 1985), I.118–29, p. 4.
2. Mark 2:1–12.
3. St. Augustine, *On the Psalms*, 41.4, quoted in *Ancient Christian Commentary of Scripture* Vol. II, eds. Thomas C. Oden and Christopher A. Hall (Downers Grove, Ill.: InterVarsity Press, 1998), p. 29.
4. Romans 12:2.

5. Romans 8:17.

6. Romans 8:37.

7. Romans 3:23–25.

8. 2 Corinthians 5:21.

9. Colin Gunton, *The Actuality of Atonement: A Study of Metaphor, Rationality, and the Christian Tradition* (Edinburgh: T&T Clark, 1988), p. 166.

10. Eric Fromm, *Escape From Freedom* (New York: Avon, 1969), p. 124.

11. Fyodor Dostoyevsky, *The Brothers Karamazov*, trans. Andrew R. MacAndrew (New York: Bantam, 1970), pp. 304–5.

12. Dante, *Purgatory*, I.70–72, p. 3.

13. Dante, *Purgatory*, I.94–98, p. 4.

14. Revelation 3:8.

15. Luke 15:1–32.

16. John 14:2–3. Some of our translations render the words "dwelling place" as "mansions," which comes from the Latin Vulgate's *mansione,* but this is misleading to the contemporary reader who associates a mansion with a very large house. Originally a *mansione* referred only to a resting place. The Greek word used by John here is *mone,* which has this same connotation of a dwelling place, a room, or a place to abide.

17. John 14:23.

18. Ezekiel 37:26–27; Zechariah 2:10.

CHAPTER 7

1. Luke 21:24.

2. Luke 9:3.

3. Dante, *Purgatory*, X.121–26, p. 111.

4. Dante, *Purgatory*, XII.124–26, p. 131.

5. Acts 8:3.

6. Philippians 3:12–14.

7. C. S. Lewis, *The Great Divorce* (New York: Macmillian, 1946), pp. 72–73.

8. Dante, *Purgatory*, X.1–3, p. 108.

9. Psalm 42:6.

10. Psalm 42:11.

11. Exodus 16:14.

12. Numbers 11:4.

13. Numbers 11:20.

14. Psalm 95:10.

CHAPTER 8

1. Psalm 25:4.

2. G. K. Chesterton, *Orthodoxy* (Colorado Springs: Shaw, 1994), p. 25.

3. Oswald Chambers, *My Utmost for His Highest* (Grand Rapids: Discovery House, 1992), March 29.

4. Here again, Dante's writing is dependent on the theological claims of Thomas Aquinas, who claimed that reason can only guide us so far before faith, by which he means the renewed will, becomes necessary to make it the rest of the way to God. Ultimately this faith is based not on reason but on revelation. But as Virgil illustrates throughout *The Divine Comedy*, and as Aquinas claimed, even rationality is an act of faithfulness that leads us far on the way home.

5. Ellen Glasgow, *The Woman Within* (New York: Harcourt Brace, 1954), p. 15.

6. Ecclesiastes 9:7.

7. Psalm 149:4.

8. Chesterton, *Orthodoxy*, pp. 12, 15.

9. Beatrice's appeal for love is solicited not only from the pilgrim's heart, but also from his mind and conscience, again like the grace of God.

10. Dante, *Purgatory*, XXXI.13–15, 88, pp. 330, 332.

11. In classical mythology this was a river of forgetfulness in Hades. Those who passed over it forgot their prior existence. Dante transforms the mythical symbol to serve as a river at the border of paradise, where past sins are washed away to oblivion.

12. Dante, *Purgatory*, XXXII.4–6, p. 343.

13. Dante, *Purgatory*, XXVIII.131–32, p. 304.

14. The allegory is also drawn from the Hebrew memory of having to cross two bodies of water in order to reach the promised land. The first was the Red Sea, in which God had parted the waters for the runaway slaves, making it obvious that it was his will for them to walk through it. But after journeying through the wilderness for forty years, the Lord expects the people to have learned how to walk by faith. So when they arrived at the Jordan River, the Hebrews were called to walk toward the unparted waters that did not divide until the soles of their feet entered. Similarly, the longer we stay on the journey with God the less obvious his direction is, and needs to be, for a people who have learned to walk by faith.

15. Dante, *Purgatory*, XXXIII.142–45, p. 362.

CHAPTER 9

1. Dante Alighieri, *The Divine Comedy: Volume III, Paradise,* trans. Mark Musa (New York: Penguin, 1986).

2. Marilyn Gardner, "What's Happening to the American Home?" *The Christian Science Monitor,* 24 July 2002.

3. John 1:1, 14.

4. G. K. Chesterton, *The Man Who Was Chesterton: The Best Essays, Stories, Poems and Other Writings of G. K. Chesterton,* ed. Raymond T. Bond (Garden City, N.Y.: Image, 1960), p. 411.

5. Matthew 8:20, Luke 9:58.

6. Acts 1:8.

7. Matthew 18:20.

8. J. Ramsey Michaels, "The Itinerant Jesus and His Home Town," *Authenticating the Activities of Jesus,* eds. Bruce Chilton and Craig Evans (Leiden, The Netherlands: Koninklijke Brill, 1999), p. 192.

9. W. D. Davies, *The Gospel and the Land: Early Christianity and Jewish Territorial Doctrine* (Berkeley: University of California Press, 1974), p. 367.

10. Ephesians 2:12–13, 19.

11. Romans 1:18–20.

12. Dante, *Paradise,* VII.28–33.

13. Colossians 1:17.

CHAPTER 10

1. Ephesians 1:3.

2. Dante, *Paradise,* XIV.28–30, p. 169.

3. Dante, *Paradise,* X.1–6, p. 119.

4. 1 John 4:16b–17.

5. Dante, *Paradise,* XXXIII.136–39, p. 394.

6. Dante, *Paradise,* XXIII.112–14, p. 274.

7. Dante, *Paradise,* I.70–72, p. 3.

8. Galatians 2:20.

9. Dante, *Paradise,* XXXI.25, p. 366.

10. Dante, *Paradise,* XXX.19–21, p. 353.

11. Dante, *Paradise,* XXXI.77–78, p. 367.

12. Dante, *Paradise,* I.103–5, 109–11, p. 4.

13. Here Dante is utilizing the Platonic belief that the material world isn't as real as the eternal ideals that lie behind it.

14. Alister McGrath, *The Unknown God: Searching for Spiritual Fulfillment* (Grand Rapids: Eerdmans, 1999), p. 85.

15. Even in his letter to the Romans, Paul claims that some are predestined (8:28–30; 9:16–24) and yet he also claims that salvation is available to all who believe (10:5–13).

16. R. W. B. Lewis, *Dante* (New York: Viking Penguin, 2001), p. 172.

17. Dante, *Paradise*, III.64–66, 70–72, 85, 88–90, pp. 34–35.

18. Bernard of Clairvaux, *On the Song of Songs*, trans. Kilian Walsh, *The Works of Bernard of Clairvaux*, vol. two (Spencer, Mass.: Cistercian Publications, 1971), 18.6, p. 138.

19. Colossians 3:1–4.

CHAPTER 11

1. Brian Tierney, *Western Europe in the Middle Ages: 300-1475* (New York: McGraw Hill, 1999), p. 271.

2. Otto von Simpson, *The Gothic Cathedral: Origins of Gothic Architecture and the Medieval Concept of Order* (Princeton: Princeton University Press, 1962), p. 61.

3. See Brian Tierney, *Western Europe in the Middle Ages*, p. 445; David Knowles and Dimitri Obolensky, *The Christian Centuries*, vol. 2 (New York: Paulist Press, 1969), p. 390.

4. M. D. Chenu, *Nature, Man, and Society in the Twelfth Century: Essays on New Theological Perspectives in the Latin West*, trans. and ed. Jerome Taylor and Lester K. Little (Chicago: University of Chicago Press, 1968), p. 5.

5. Robert Wuthnow, *After Heaven: Spirituality in America Since the 1950s* (Berkeley: University of California Press, 1998), p. 168.

6. Thomas Moore, *Care of the Soul: A Guide for Cultivating Depth and Sacredness in Everyday Life* (New York: Harper Collins, 1992), pp. 66–67.

7. Moore, *Care of the Soul*, p. xvii.

8. Dante, *Paradise*, VII.85–88, p. 85.

9. Dante, *Paradise*, VII.112–20, pp. 85–86.

10. Dante, *Paradise*, VII.106–8, p. 85.

11. The early church had been celebrating Communion since the moment Christ initiated the sacrament. By the end of the first century it was clear that the church celebrated this sacrament every week, and made it the center point of their worship services. It long predated the regular exposition of Scriptures in a sermon. But around the beginning of the fourth century when Christianity was transformed from a persecuted faith into the state religion of the empire, monasticism became the primary means of exercising spirituality for close to a thousand years. Anselm obviously didn't initiate the Catholic Mass, but his renewal of its theology returned the primary locus of church spirituality to the altar.

12. 1 Corinthians 15:19.

13. Dante, *Paradise*, XIV.19–30, p. 169.

14. Dante, *Paradise,* XXXIII.142–45, p. 394.